THE
MIRACULOUS MEDAL

BOOKS BY MARY FABYAN WINDEATT

In This Series

Stories of the Saints for Young People ages 10 to 100

THE CHILDREN OF FATIMA
And Our Lady's Message to the World

THE CURÉ OF ARS
The Story of St. John Vianney,
Patron Saint of Parish Priests

THE LITTLE FLOWER
The Story of St. Therese of the Child Jesus

PATRON SAINT OF FIRST COMMUNICANTS
The Story of Blessed Imelda Lambertini

THE MIRACULOUS MEDAL
The Story of Our Lady's Appearances
to St. Catherine Labouré

ST. LOUIS DE MONTFORT
The Story of Our Lady's Slave,
St. Louis Mary Grignion De Montfort

THE
MIRACULOUS MEDAL

THE STORY OF
OUR LADY'S APPEARANCES TO
SAINT CATHERINE LABOURÉ

By
Mary Fabyan Windeatt

Illustrated by
Gedge Harmon

TAN BOOKS AND PUBLISHERS, INC.
Rockford, Illinois 61105

Nihil Obstat: Francis J. Reine, S.T.D.
                     Censor Librorum

Imprimatur: ✠ Paul C. Schulte, D.D.
                     Archbishop of Indianapolis
                     November 27, 1949
                     Feast of Our Lady
                        of the Miraculous Medal

First published in 1950, as "A Grail Publication," at St. Meinrad, Indiana,
under the title *The Medal: The Story of Saint Catherine Labouré.*

ISBN: 0-89555-417-8

Library of Congress Catalog Card No.:   90-71823

Printed and bound in the United States of America.

TAN BOOKS AND PUBLISHERS, INC.
P.O.Box 424
Rockford, Illinois 61105
1991

To all who wear
The Miraculous Medal
(the Medal of the Immaculate Conception
of the Blessed Virgin Mary)—
and especially to those
who make known its power for grace.

CONTENTS

1. Our Lady Comes to Sister Catherine....... 1

2. Father Aladel Does Not Believe........... 6

3. The Vision of the Medal................. 11

4. Father Aladel Still Hesitates.............. 16

5. Father Aladel Finally Consents............ 21

6. The Bishop Says Yes..................... 26

7. Finding the Right Picture................ 30

8. The Medal Becomes Known as
   "The Miraculous Medal"............... 34

9. Obstinate Old John...................... 39

10. Sister Catherine Continues Her Story...... 45

11. Old John Finally Agrees to Wear the Medal. 49

12. The Graces People Forget to Ask For...... 54

13. Old John Decides to Go to Confession..... 59

14. The Children of Mary................... 64

15. Our Lady Converts an Anti-Catholic Jew.... 69

16. The Rays................................ 76

17. "The Streets Will Run with Blood"........ 81

18. A New Request from Our Lady.......... 86

19. A Disappointing Trip..................... 91

20. Sister Catherine Breaks Her Long Silence... 95

21. Sister Catherine's Last Request............101

   Note on St. Catherine Laboure's
      Canonization........................107

THE
MIRACULOUS MEDAL

OUR LADY COMES TO
SISTER CATHERINE

CHAPTER 1

HE lights of the great city of Paris flickered and gleamed like so many jewels in the darkness of the soft July night. Gay music drifted from the sidewalk cafes, and an endless stream of carriages rolled up and down the broad avenues on their way from the theaters. But at the Motherhouse of the Daughters of Charity all was silence. The Sisters were fast asleep, after a hard day's work in preparation for the Feast of Saint Vincent de Paul, who had founded their Society some two hundred years before. The next day would be one of joyful celebration at the convent.

Like the other religious, young Sister Labouré had fallen into the sound sleep of exhaustion. Then presently she stirred uneasily. Was someone calling her?

With a start she sat up. The dormitory was in darkness, yet surely a light was moving outside the white curtains surrounding her bed? And yes—someone *had* called her! She now heard her name spoken for the third time.

Quickly she parted the curtains, looked out, then drew back in astonishment. A few feet away stood

1

a little boy about five years old—blue-eyed, golden-haired—dressed in shining white garments!

"Come to the chapel," he invited. "The Blessed Virgin is waiting for you."

Sister Labouré could scarcely believe her eyes, or her ears. The chapel? At this hour of the night? The ... *the Blessed Virgin?*

The child seemed to read her thoughts. "Don't be afraid," he said. "It's half-past eleven. Everyone's asleep. Come along. I'll wait for you."

With trembling fingers Sister Labouré began to dress. Was all this a dream? Oh, surely not! Ever since she had been a little girl she had prayed to see the Blessed Virgin. And now, on the eve of the Feast of Saint Vincent de Paul. . . .

In just a few minutes she was ready. The little boy was waiting for her as he had promised, and at once the two set off for the chapel. As they hurried down the empty corridors, the young Sister's astonishment grew by leaps and bounds. All the lights were burning! And when they reached the chapel, the heavy doors swung open at the mere touch of the child's hand to reveal still more lights and all the altar candles ablaze.

"It's just as though there were going to be Midnight Mass!" thought Sister Labouré excitedly.

Without hesitation the child moved up the center aisle of the chapel into the sanctuary, then came to a stop before an arm chair where the chaplain was accustomed to sit while addressing the community. Sister Labouré's heart pounded with excitement as

THE CHAPEL WAS ABLAZE WITH LIGHTS.

she knelt down at the altar rail and looked eagerly about. The Blessed Virgin! Where was she?

But as the minutes passed and nothing happened, Sister Labouré grew uneasy. She looked at the child standing a few feet away, then turned to gaze anxiously about the chapel. Suppose someone were to see her! It could so easily happen that one of the Sisters, on duty with the sick, might be attracted by the lights. . . .

Then suddenly the child made a sign. "Here is the Blessed Virgin," he said.

Even as he spoke there was a rustling of silk, and Sister Labouré's eyes grew wide with wonder. Coming down from the right side of the altar and advancing gracefully toward the arm chair was the most beautiful lady that she had ever seen! But . . . *was she the Blessed Virgin?* Her yellowish-white dress and blue veil were much like what Saint Anne was wearing in a picture that was hanging in the sanctuary. Then, even the chair and the way the beautiful stranger seated herself in it. . . .

As though reading her thoughts, the child nodded reassuringly. "Yes, it's the Blessed Virgin," he said.

Yet Sister Labouré remained full of misgivings. Was she really awake, or was this a dream? Could it be that the beautiful one sitting in the chair was some great lady, a friend of the convent? She felt unable to speak or stir.

As she continued to kneel stupidly where she was, the child seemed to lose all patience. "It *is* the

Blessed Virgin!" he exclaimed, and now his voice was deep and stern, like that of a man. "Go to her! Can't you see that she is waiting for you?"

At these words, all doubts vanished. Sister Labouré hurried forward into the sanctuary and knelt by the arm chair, her hands upon the Blessed Virgin's knees.

"Mother!" she cried joyfully, looking up into the gracious face turned to hers. "You've really come!"

The heavenly one smiled. "Yes," she said, and her voice was like the sweetest music. "I've come."

FATHER ALADEL DOES NOT BELIEVE

CHAPTER 2

N ALL her twenty-four years, Sister Labouré had never been so happy as at this
moment. How beautiful the Blessed
Virgin was! How kind! How... how
motherly! Yet there was also a certain
sadness. ...

"My child, you, too, will know sadness," said Our
Lady gently. "But in time of trial, come here before
the altar and pour out all your troubles. Then you
will receive every consolation."

Sister Labouré was silent. Troubles! How far
away they seemed now! Yet of course she would remember these words of the Blessed Virgin. And
her other words, too.

"My child, the good God wishes to charge you with
a mission. You will have much to suffer, but you
will bear it all with the thought that you are doing
it for His glory. You will understand what the good
God desires, and it will trouble you only until you
make it known to him who has to direct you. You
will be contradicted, but you will also have the
graces you need. Do not doubt it. Speak with confidence and simplicity. Fear not."

The Blessed Virgin continued to speak, telling Sister Labouré that dreadful times were in store for France. The government would be overthrown by evil men. Priests and nuns would be persecuted. The Archbishop of Paris would lose his life. But the Daughters of Charity and the Priests of the Mission —the two communities which Saint Vincent de Paul had founded—were not to be afraid. They would be protected by .the Blessed Virgin herself. And many special graces would be given to all—religious and laity—who would ask for them.

Suddenly, as strangely as she had come, the Blessed Virgin vanished. Scarcely knowing what she did, Sister Labouré rose from her knees and looked about the sanctuary. There, standing a few feet away, was the little boy.

"She's gone," he said softly. And coming toward her, he indicated that they should go, too.

As though in a dream, Sister Labouré obediently accompanied her small guide down the main aisle of the chapel and back to the dormitory. When he also vanished without warning, she made ready for bed again. But as the clock struck two, she knew that sleep was impossible. What a marvelous night—this night of July 18, 1830! For two hours she had seen and spoken with the Mother of God! What was there to do now but relive every minute of that glorious interview?

Then suddenly a troublesome thought entered her mind. The Blessed Virgin had said that God wished to charge her with a mission—a special work. But there had been no mention of what it might be.

"And I forgot to ask!" thought Sister Labouré in dismay.

But soon she had comforted herself. Surely Father Aladel, the convent chaplain, would be able to help. After all, she was to tell him—and no one else —of everything that had happened during the past two hours.

"Yes, that's it," she reflected. "Father Aladel will know what to do."

But when Sister Labouré informed the chaplain of the Blessed Virgin's visit, his response was most discouraging. In fact, he dismissed the whole affair as childish nonsense.

"Sister, either you had a dream or you have too much imagination," he declared. "Forget about the whole thing."

"But Father!" protested Sister Labouré in dismay. "The Blessed Virgin *did* come! And my guardian angel, too!"

"*Your guardian angel?*"

"Yes, I'm sure that's who the little boy was. Oh, Father, ever since I was very small I've prayed to him to let me see the Blessed Virgin! Now, don't you understand? He's finally heard my prayer."

For a long moment Father Aladel was silent. Never in all his thirty years had he met anyone— even the holiest priest or religious—who believed that he or she had seen and spoken with the Mother of God. Yet here was a young woman (a novice at

"GOD WISHES TO CHARGE YOU WITH A MISSION."

the Motherhouse for scarcely three months) who announced with the most alarming eagerness that the great privilege had been hers.

"Sister, don't think any more about it," he advised hurriedly. "Things such as you've told me . . . well, one must be very careful about them."

Sister Labouré said no more. The work which the Blessed Virgin had told her God wanted her to do—plainly, Father Aladel knew nothing about it. Nor did he appear to want to know anything about it. And since he was her confessor and represented Christ Himself. . . .

"All right, Father. I'll try to forget about everything," she promised. Then, after a pause: "But oh—how beautiful it all was! How . . . how *good!*"

THE VISION OF THE MEDAL

CHAPTER 3

F COURSE Father Aladel did not mean to be unkind to Sister Labouré. However, he realized only too well that sometimes good people, even very good people, believe that they have seen and heard heavenly things, only to discover later that they have imagined everything. Then, what embarrassment for everyone concerned! What scandal!

To make matters more complicated, this was not the first time that Sister Labouré had come to him with a startling tale. Only three months ago, when she had been at the convent just a few days, she had told him that she had seen the heart of Saint Vincent de Paul floating in the air over the silver box in the chapel containing his relics! Then, a week or so later, that she had seen Our Lord while assisting at Mass!

"The poor child is trying so hard to be holy that she really believes she has visions," he decided. "The wisest thing to do is to pay no attention to her stories."

Sister Labouré was disappointed in Father Aladel's disbelief in what she told him. But remembering the words of the Blessed Virgin—that in time of trial she was to come before the altar and pour out all her troubles—she did not worry too much.

"Dear Lord, please help me!" she begged, as she knelt before the Tabernacle. "And please tell me what it is that I'm to do for You."

Months went by, and it began to seem as though these prayers were not to be answered. Yet Sister Labouré did not give up hope. What had Our Lady told her on the night of July 18, the eve of the Feast of Saint Vincent de Paul?

"My child, the good God wishes to charge you with a mission. You will have much to suffer, but you will bear it all with the thought that you are doing it for His glory...."

A mission! A special work for souls! Oh, surely the Blessed Virgin herself would come again to explain?

Then suddenly Sister Labouré's hope was rewarded. Late in the afternoon on Saturday, November 27, while she was at meditation with the other religious in the chapel, she heard the same sound which she had heard on that wonderful night more than four months ago: the rustle of silk. Eagerly she looked toward the sanctuary whence it came. Then her heart gave a great leap. There, standing close to a picture of Saint Joseph, and upon what seemed to be a shining globe, was the Blessed Virgin!

How beautiful she was! Even more beautiful than on her first visit! Her simple, flowing dress resembled the color of the sky at dawn—a radiant white, shot through with shimmering gold. A white veil covered her head, falling gracefully to her feet, and in her hands she held a small golden ball, surmounted with a cross, which she pressed lovingly to her heart.

Sister Labouré gazed in ecstasy at the marvelous sight, quite heedless of the other Sisters around her. Then suddenly she noticed that the Virgin's fingers were glistening with numerous brilliant rings. The stones in these rings sent forth such dazzling rays that one could scarcely bear to look upon them. Indeed, they enveloped the Blessed Virgin in so much splendor that neither her feet nor her robe could be seen. And yet some of the precious stones were not sending forth any rays. . . .

What did it all mean? Sister Labouré did not even try to understand. It was enough that the Blessed Virgin had come again; that she was standing only a few yards away, her eyes lifted to heaven with an expression of indescribable love. Then suddenly she lowered her eyes and looked directly at Sister Labouré. And though her lips did not move, there was no mistaking the sound of her voice:

"The globe which you see represents the world, especially France, and everyone in it. The rays are the symbol of the graces I shed on those who ask me for them." Then, after a pause: "The stones which send forth no light represent the graces for which people forget to ask me."

Suddenly the golden ball which the Blessed Virgin was holding vanished. She lowered her hands, and the brilliant rays shone forth with even greater

"HAVE A MEDAL MADE AFTER THIS MODEL."

splendor. A moment later an oval frame appeared about her, with an inscription in golden letters: *O Mary, conceived without sin, pray for us who have recourse to thee.* Then, to Sister Labouré's astonishment, a heavenly voice spoke within the depths of her own heart:

"Have a medal made after this model," it said. "All who wear it after it has been blessed will receive great graces, especially if they wear it around the neck. Graces will abound for those who wear it with confidence."

Presently the vision seemed to turn around, revealing a letter M, surmounted by a cross and a bar. Beneath the M were the Hearts of Jesus and Mary— the first, crowned with thorns, the other pierced by a sword, and the whole encircled by twelve stars.

Sister Labouré gazed in an ecstasy of joy. To have a medal made like this in honor of the Blessed Virgin! It was the mission—the special work for souls—which God wanted of her. . . .

CHAPTER 4

OOR Father Aladel was beside himself with worry when he heard the story of Our Lady's second appearance.

"Sister, it *couldn't* have happened!" he declared emphatically. "It was all a dream like the other time."

But Sister Labouré shook her head with childlike confidence. "Oh, no, Father! I saw the Blessed Virgin as plainly as I see you, for it was still daylight in the chapel. And she wants the medal made right away so that people can wear it and start earning graces."

"But ... but that's impossible!"

Sister Labouré looked up in astonishment. "Impossible? But why, Father?"

"Because neither you nor I have the right to undertake such a work."

"But the Blessed Virgin said...."

"Nonsense. Forget the whole thing. Just say your prayers and try to be like the other Sisters. After all, aren't you just a novice?"

"Yes, Father."

"And isn't a novice supposed to do what her Superiors tell her?"

"Oh, yes, Father."

"Very well, then. Don't let me hear any more

16

about these visions. Or this foolishness about having a special medal made, either. It's dangerous to give your attention to such fancies."

Obediently Sister Labouré promised to put the thought of Our Lady's visits out of her mind. But a month later she came to Father Aladel, her eyes shining with joy.

"Father, I've seen her again—in the chapel!" she burst out. "And she's really in earnest about having the medal made."

With an effort the young priest controlled his impatience, consoled by the thought that in a few weeks Sister Labouré would complete her novitiate at the Motherhouse in Paris and be sent to work in some other convent. What a relief to hear no more of these stories!

Nevertheless he realized that he must not be too harsh toward Sister Labouré. After all, she had made a good record as a novice. She was cheerful, hard-working, obedient, trustworthy. . . .

"Well, Sister, if the Blessed Virgin really came again, what did she look like this time?" he asked in a matter-of-fact voice. "And what did she say to you?"

Sister Labouré's heart filled with happiness. Was Father Aladel beginning to understand at last?

"She seemed to be about forty years old, Father. And just as beautiful as ever, with the rings on her fingers sending out the rays, and her dress—oh, it's impossible to describe it!"

"I suppose it was blue?"

"No, Father. It was white, and very plainly made, but somehow it shone like the sun. And the oval frame was there again, too, with the little prayer inside: *O Mary, conceived without sin, pray for us who have recourse to thee.*"

"You saw all this in the chapel?"

"Yes, Father. Only this time it was in a different place."

"Our Lady wasn't sitting in the arm chair? Or standing by Saint Joseph's picture?"

"No, this time she passed by Saint Joseph's picture and went up behind the altar, to stand above the Tabernacle—just as though she were a statue. Then, after a little while...."

"Yes?"

"The whole picture seemed to turn around, just like the other time, and I saw the two hearts."

"One with thorns around it and the other pierced by a sword?"

"Yes, the Hearts of Jesus and Mary. Then the twelve stars were there, too. Oh, Father, you know what this means, don't you?"

"What, Sister?"

"Why, it's the back of the medal! Our Lady is to be on the front, just as I've described her to you— holding out her hands with the rays coming from them. But on the back there are to be the two hearts and the letter M, with the cross and the bar on top. *And* the twelve stars. Oh, Father! How soon do you think the medal can be ready?"

The priest's heart sank. What a dreadful state of

IT WAS THE BACK OF THE MEDAL.

affairs! Because he had refrained from ridiculing the third vision, Sister Labouré seemed to feel that he believed in it. Even worse. She was acting as though he had every intention of having the medal made without delay.

"Sister. . . ." he began, then stopped. Something must be done, and at once, otherwise he would have no peace. But what? Then suddenly the answer came.

"Sister, what writing should be put on the back of the medal?" he demanded sharply.

Sister Labouré's eyes opened wide in astonishment. "*Writing*, Father?"

"Yes. You say the front of the medal has the prayer: *O Mary, conceived without sin, pray for us who have recourse to thee.* Well, surely there should be another prayer on the back?"

For a moment the young nun was silent. Then she shook her head doubtfully. "I don't think there should be any prayer, Father. At least, I don't remember seeing anything. . . ."

Quickly Father Aladel seized his chance. "Well, we can't do a thing about the medal until we're sure —absolutely sure—what the Blessed Virgin wants," he declared. "That's certain. So for the time being we'll not make any plans."

Sister Labouré clasped her hands anxiously. "But Father! How can we find out what the Blessed Virgin wants?"

The priest shrugged his shoulders. "Why, by asking her, of course. The next time she comes."

CHAPTER 5

 FEW weeks later—in January, 1831— with the other novices, Sister Labouré was permitted to make her religious vows and to receive the habit of a Daughter of Charity. And to show that she was really entering upon a new life—with all her actions taking on an added merit because she now belonged to God in a special way—she was given a new name: that of Catherine.

Of course Sister Catherine was happy beyond words. At last she was a religious—a Daughter of Saint Vincent de Paul! Oh, how good to belong to a family whose special work was the care of the poor and sick! But even as she rejoiced, Sister Catherine was bothered by a nagging worry. The medal had not been made. Nor could it be made until the Blessed Virgin announced what words she wished to have appear on the back.

"Dearest Mother, please tell me!" was Sister Catherine's constant prayer.

Without any warning the answer came. One day while kneeling in the chapel, the young religious

21

heard a voice speaking within the depths of her soul: "The letter M and the two Hearts are enough."

Sister Catherine was filled with relief and joy. The Blessed Virgin had come again! True, this time she was not visible in her beautiful dress of white and gold, with the dazzling rays streaming from her outstretched hands. But her voice—oh, there was no mistaking it! So gentle, so kind... *so loving!*

"Oh, Mother, thank you!" she burst out. "Now we can surely do something about having the medal made."

But when Sister Catherine sought out Father Aladel to tell him of Our Lady's message, the young priest was just as doubtful as ever. Nor was he impressed by the fact that Sister Catherine was about to leave the Motherhouse for a new home—a convent of the Daughters of Charity at Enghien, a suburb of Paris—and that she was desperately eager to carry out Our Lady's wishes before her departure.

"Sister, there's no hurry about any of this," he declared. "In fact, I think that the longer we wait, the better."

Sister Catherine was beside herself with dismay. "But it's more than six months since the Blessed Virgin came the first time, Father! And two months since she first spoke about the medal...."

The priest shrugged his shoulders. "Six months! Two months! Sister, what is that in the light of eternity? Nothing! Absolutely nothing!"

Sister Catherine hesitated. "But Father! At Enghien I won't be able to see you very often. And

ONE DAY SHE HEARD OUR LADY'S VOICE.

if the Blessed Virgin should have another message. . . ."

The priest nodded reassuringly. "Don't worry," he said. "Enghien isn't far away. I'll come to see you every so often."

True enough. In the months that followed Father Aladel paid several visits to the convent at Enghien, where Sister Catherine was busily engaged in the kitchen. But despite her evident certainty, he still could not bring himself to believe that the Mother of God had actually appeared to his young friend in the chapel of the Motherhouse in Paris, and that she wished to have a special medal made. And yet, he reflected in a puzzled way, Sister Catherine was not the sort of person who would stoop to telling lies. She was humble, prayerful, hard-working, obedient. . . .

"And sensible, too," he was forced to admit, "not in the least inclined to day-dream or show off. It's beyond me," he always concluded.

Then one day in the year 1832 Sister Catherine announced that she had heard Our Lady's voice again (although she had not seen her), and that the Virgin was very disappointed because the medal had not been made.

"I told her it wasn't my fault, Father—that somehow you can't bring yourself to believe me. And do you know what she said?"

The priest shook his head, looking rather anxious. "What, Sister?"

" 'Don't worry. A day will come when Father Aladel will do what I wish. He is my servant, and would fear to displease me.' "

At these words a chill settled over the young priest's heart. What a thought—that he would willingly disobey the Blessed Virgin! That perhaps even now, because of his doubts and hesitation during the past two years, she was displeased with him!

"Sister, this settles it," he declared abruptly. "I'll go to see the Archbishop at once. If he approves of the medal, we'll have it made without any more delay."

CHAPTER 6

O THE amazement of Father Aladel, the Archbishop of Paris offered not the slightest objection to having the medal made. Nor did he express any doubts that the Blessed Virgin had appeared to one of the Daughters of Charity in the chapel at the Motherhouse.

"Who is the Sister?" he inquired eagerly. "I must see her at once."

Father Etienne, who had accompanied Father Aladel to the Archbishop's house, waited with bated breath. Since he occupied a position of authority among the Priests of the Mission (the religious family to which Father Aladel belonged), the latter had already told him a few details of Our Lady's visits. Now, in the presence of the Archbishop, surely the whole amazing story would be forthcoming.

But Father Aladel shook his head regretfully. "Your Grace, I can't tell you who the Sister is," he said. "Nor can I allow anyone to question her. It's the one thing she made me promise."

The eyes of the Archbishop clouded with disappointment. "But Father! This Sister must be a saint! Surely it wouldn't hurt to have a visit with her . . . to hear her own account of these visions. . . ."

26

As respectfully as he could, Father Aladel repeated that this could not be. Our Lady had told the Sister in question that she was to confide in no one save the priest who heard her Confession.

"But if we can't see or talk to the Sister, how are we going to make plans for the medal?" objected the Archbishop. "Surely an artist will have to talk to her about the various details."

"Yes," put in Father Etienne. "There'll have to be several sketches before anything definite can be decided."

For a moment Father Aladel was silent. The same thorny problem that had been bothering him! Sister Catherine had not the slightest ability to draw or paint, and neither had he.

"Perhaps I could talk to the artist," he suggested finally. "From what's been told to me in confidence, I've a fair idea of how the Blessed Virgin looked on her various visits. If you're really in earnest about the medal, Your Grace. . . ."

The Archbishop replied with decision. "Father, I couldn't be more in earnest about anything," he said. "These are dangerous days, not only for France but the whole world. Why, actually it's not safe for me to walk in the streets!"

The two priests exchanged an understanding glance. It was true. Two years ago a serious revolution had broken out in France. The Emperor had been dethroned and a group of godless men had taken over the government. To date, the Daughters of Charity had been permitted to continue their work,

"FIND AN ARTIST AT ONCE, FATHER."

for it was well known how good and necessary their hospitals and orphanages were. Generally speaking, the Priests of the Mission had been let alone, too. But many other religious groups had been cruelly persecuted, and for several months there had been such threats against the life of the Archbishop that he had been forced to go into hiding.

"You mean it's all right to go ahead, Your Grace?" asked Father Aladel. "To find an artist and have some sketches made to show the Sister?"

The Archbishop raised his hand in blessing. "Find an artist at once, Father. To my way of thinking, this medal—through Our Lady's merits—can mean the saving of France. Perhaps even of the whole world!"

FINDING THE RIGHT PICTURE

CHAPTER 7

HEN Father Aladel took his departure, he felt that the burden of anxiety which he had carried for so long had been wonderfully removed from him. Without delay he set out in search of an artist willing to undertake the task of making the medal, and in due course such a man was found. But in just a few days it became apparent that this was to be no simple matter. For instance, on November 27, 1830, Our Lady had appeared to Sister Catherine, dressed in a simple white robe and holding a small golden ball surmounted with a cross. She had lovingly pressed this ball to her heart, then raised it toward heaven, as though she were offering it to God.

But then the ball had vanished. She had lowered her hands and stood facing the Sister, the beautiful rings on her fingers (some bright with dazzling rays, others without any radiance), turned away from view, but with a glorious light still streaming from her open palms.

"Father, what about this?" demanded the artist. "The ball was no longer in Our Lady's hands when

30

she said she wanted the medal made. But surely it has some special meaning and should be shown?"

The young priest hesitated. Undoubtedly the ball did have a special meaning. In fact, it represented the world. But since it had vanished when Our Lady had asked to have the medal made. . . .

"You'd better make two sketches," he told the artist. "The Sister will know which one to choose."

But the artist was quick to discover more difficulties. Our Lady had been seen standing on a shining globe. Well, was the whole of this visible, or only part? Then, were her feet bare or covered? And was the Devil to be shown under her feet in the form of a snake? As for her hair, was it entirely hidden by the long veil?

Presently the confused and rather exasperated priest had a whole series of drawings to take to Enghien to show to Sister Catherine, in the hope that she could shed some light on the artist's seemingly insoluble problems. And how eagerly she examined each one, delighted beyond words that at last something was being done about Our Lady's request.

Father Aladel watched her closely. Which drawing would she choose? Suddenly she gave a gasp of pleasure.

"Father, this is it!" she cried, holding up one of the drawings. "Have the medal made like this!"

The priest leaned forward. The sketch which Sister Catherine had chosen did not show the golden ball. Instead, Our Lady was standing with outstretched hands atop a cloud-encircled globe, the rays

"FATHER, THIS IS IT!"

from her open palms streaming earthwards in a blaze of glory. Her hair was covered, her feet bare, crushing beneath them an evil-looking serpent.

"The rays represent the graces she wants to give us!" explained Sister Catherine eagerly. "Oh, Father! I could spend hours just looking at those rays and thinking about them!"

For a moment Father Aladel was silent. What wisdom was here! Since the first Good Friday the Blessed Virgin had been the mother of the world. But, save for a few devout priests and religious, who was there to remember? Or that she had done everything for her Son and would do everything for her other children—*if only they would ask her help?*

"Sister, you're right," he acknowledged, gazing reverently at the sketch. "The rays from Our Lady's hands do represent every kind of blessing. And if the new medal will make people understand this. ..."

"Oh, it will, Father! I know it will!" exclaimed Sister Catherine confidently. "After all, remember what she told me?"

"What, Sister?"

" 'All who wear the medal after it has been blessed will receive great graces, especially if they wear it around the neck. Graces will abound for those who wear it with confidence.' "

Suddenly a joy that he had never known before filled Father Aladel's heart. How good to have a part to play in bringing souls to love and trust God's Mother—*and theirs!*

THE MEDAL BECOMES KNOWN AS "THE MIRACULOUS MEDAL"

CHAPTER 8

 OON the first medals were ready—two thousand of them. But despite his conviction that their inspiration came from heaven, Father Aladel was worried. The new medals were beautiful, yes. But had it been wise to have so many made? Perhaps a thousand... or even only five hundred....

"It's all right, Father," said the Archbishop. "The medal is a special gift from the Blessed Virgin. I know that people are going to want it."

True enough. Within a short time the story of how Our Lady had appeared to one of the Daughters of Charity was making the rounds in Paris, and the supply of medals was quickly exhausted. Then interest spread to other cities, and several thousand more had to be made. And when it was observed that those who wore the new medal were marvelously preserved from the cholera plague which had recently broken out—even to the point of being cured when they were on the verge of death—excitement reached fever pitch.

"The medal is miraculous!" one person told another eagerly. "It isn't safe to be without it."

Naturally the Daughters of Charity were among the first to distribute "The Miraculous Medal." They

THE SISTERS GAVE THE MEDAL TO THEIR ORPHANS.

gave them to their orphans, to the sick in their hospitals, to the poor and aged under their care. But even as they worked to promote an interest in Our Lady's cause, all were asking themselves the same question: *Who is the Sister to whom Our Lady appeared?*

"It's Sister Martha," several decided. "She's a real saint."

"No, it's Sister Victoria. She's always had a wonderful devotion to the Blessed Virgin."

"Don't forget Sister Pauline. She's very holy."

"Well, what about Sister Marie? Have you ever watched her pray?"

"Yes. But there's something about Sister Anne. . . ."

"Nonsense. Our Lady came to Sister Genevieve. . . ."

"Oh, no! It must be Sister Claire. . . ."

At the convent of the Daughters of Charity at Enghien (where Sister Catherine was still employed in the kitchen), there was as much curiosity as anywhere else. Even the fifty homeless old men who were the Sisters' special charge joined in the guessing game. But as the weeks passed, not even those who were most positive in expressing their opinions could actually be sure who the privileged soul was. Even the Superior and the chaplain could only guess, like the rest. As for Sister Catherine—busy with peeling potatoes, scrubbing the pots and pans, feeding the chickens—she calmly contributed her guesses to those of the others when the occasion arose.

"It could be Sister Martha," she would say, when pressed for an opinion. *"Or* Sister Pauline. *Or* Sister Marie. . . ."

However, Sister Catherine was far more interested in promoting a love of Our Lady than in idle talk about the apparitions in the chapel of the Motherhouse. Two things in particular were of concern to her: first, that the beautiful prayer, *O Mary, conceived without sin, pray for us who have recourse to thee,* be recited frequently and devoutly by all who wore the medal; second, that the medal itself be worn about the neck.

Now there were a few old men at Enghien who did not want to wear the medal about their necks. They preferred to carry it in a pocket, or to have it pinned to their clothing. In this way, they would not be advertising their piety.

"It's all right for women to wear the medal openly," they said. "It's something like jewelry. But men—well, it's different with them."

Sister Catherine was not surprised at such an attitude. For many years the Church had been cruelly persecuted in France. Even now the godless ones in charge of the government were doing their best to banish it from the land—if not by outright violence, at least by mockery and ridicule. As a result, there was little public interest in religion, and only a few people were to be found praying in the churches. As for rosaries, statues and holy pictures in the homes —they were scarcely ever to be seen.

"People are ashamed of the Faith and everything connected with it," thought Sister Catherine. "That's why the Blessed Virgin said her medal would bring far greater graces if worn about the neck."

What should be done—especially with regard to those old men at Enghien who were so reluctant to pay public tribute to the Mother of God? For weeks Sister Catherine prayed and thought about the matter. Well did she know there was no use in *making* anyone wear the medal. It would be well-nigh impossible, and it could do more harm than good.

"I'll just have to gain their confidence," she decided finally. "Dearest Mother, won't you please help me?"

OBSTINATE OLD JOHN

CHAPTER 9

O HER prayers for this intention, Sister Catherine added sacrifices of all sorts. Nothing was too hard or too much trouble to win the grace which she so ardently desired for all those living at Enghien: namely, that they should acquire a real love of the Blessed Virgin. Then one morning. . . .

"Sister, old John is quite sick," the Superior announced. "He's had another spell. But he wants to talk to you."

Sister Catherine stared in amazement. Old John was one of the most obstinate of all the men living at Enghien. From the start he had refused to have anything to do with the medal. Moreover, for years he had caused the Sisters great distress by his habit of using bad language and his refusal to go to the Sacraments. Now. . . .

"John wants to see *me*, Mother? The cook?"

"Yes. You'd better go at once."

So Sister Catherine hurried off to the infirmary, where she found John tossing in a high fever. Any expectations that his request for her might mean a change of heart were quickly dashed. He was, in fact, more disagreeable than usual.

39

"Sister, everyone here is stupid and clumsy," he grumbled. "I'm not being looked after right. I want you to be my nurse."

Sister Catherine sat down by the bed. She was more than busy in the kitchen, but if there was something she could do for this poor fellow. . . .

"All right, John," she said, smiling. "What would you like? Some water? Another pillow? Or maybe your bed could be moved a little."

John grunted impatiently. "No, no. I just want you to tell me a story. And not any foolishness about saints or angels, either. I'm tired of hearing about them."

A pang shot through Sister Catherine's heart. Poor John! The Devil was trying so hard to win his soul. And barring a miracle, the struggle would be over without warning; John would die without the Sacraments.

"But I don't know any stories except holy ones, John. After all, they're really the best."

The old man's face grew hard. "Holy stories!" he muttered impatiently. "They're all right for children, Sister, but not for me. Tell me something interesting. About yourself, for instance."

"Myself?"

"Yes. Your family, your friends, where you were born, why you came here . . . anything!"

Sister Catherine's heart sank. She had no desire to talk about herself. Her one desire was to bring souls to a knowledge and a love of the Blessed Virgin. Still, she *had* prayed to win the confidence of everyone at Enghien in order to spread devotion to the Miraculous Medal. And perhaps if she satisfied John's childish whim. . . .

"All right. I'll tell you something about myself," she said, and with some reluctance launched into her story—beginning with the birth of Zoe Catherine Labouré, the ninth of eleven children, on May 2, 1806, at Fain-les-Moutiers, a village in the province of Burgundy.

"I grew up on my father's farm, John, and was very happy. But when I was nine years old, Mother died. Oh, what a blow that was! But then I decided to ask the Blessed Virgin to be my mother. . . ."

At once the sick man sat bolt upright. "Sister!" he roared. "Remember what I said? No holy stories!"

Sister Catherine had to smile, in spite of herself. "But wait, John! It's all part of what happened to me as a child. Don't you want to hear the rest of it?"

For a moment John glared. Then, slowly, he settled back on his pillow. "Well . . . all right," he muttered. "Go on."

"There was a statue of the Blessed Virgin in the kitchen. When I thought no one was looking, I climbed upon a chair and took it in my arms. 'Now *you* will be my mother,' I said. '*You* will look after me.' And she did, John! From that very day!"

The sick man shut his eyes. "Humph!" he grunted. "I suppose the Blessed Virgin moved right into your father's house, and did the cooking and the washing and the mending!"

"NOW **YOU** WILL BE MY MOTHER!"

"No. But she did see to it that the neighbors should be very kind. And that Aunt Marguerite should take my little sister and me to live with her for the next two years. And when my big brothers left home to make their way in the world, she looked after them, too."

Once again there was silence, and after a moment Sister Catherine saw fit to resume her story—relating countless little incidents that she thought might be of interest.

As was to be expected, John interrupted from time to time—especially when the story took a religious turn. Noting this, Sister Catherine briefly passed over the entrance into the Daughters of Charity of her older sister Marie Louise. But when it came time to tell of her own vocation....

"John, when I was twelve years old I knew I wanted to be a religious. But my father wouldn't hear of it. Not even when I was eighteen years old would he allow me to leave for the convent. Then one night I had the strangest dream. I seemed to be in church, assisting at the Mass of a kindly old priest. When all was over, he beckoned to me to come to him. But I was too frightened, and ran away. Later, I seemed to be at the house of a sick person, and there was the old priest again.

" 'My child, it's a wonderful thing to care for the sick,' he told me. 'You avoid me just now, but a day will come when you will seek me out. God expects something from you. Don't forget that.' "

"Once again I was terrified, and ran away as fast as I could. Then—what do you think?"

There was no answer, and Sister Catherine leaned forward anxiously. But almost at once she relaxed. Wonder of wonders! John had fallen into a healthful sleep!

For a moment she looked at him, then took a Miraculous Medal from her pocket. Well she knew that it would never do to place it about his neck. When he awoke, he might be so angry that he would have a stroke. But surely there would be no harm in leaving it somewhere in the room ... perhaps under the mattress. ...

"Dearest Mother, please help this poor man!" she begged silently. "Bring him to know and love you and your Son ... *soon!*"

SISTER CATHERINE CONTINUES HER STORY

CHAPTER 10

ATE that afternoon Sister Catherine's kitchen duties were interrupted for a second time. After several hours of refreshing sleep, old John was awake and asking for her.

"He seems to be much better," said the Superior, eyeing Sister Catherine in a curious fashion. "Believe me, if you've done anything to help that troublesome old man...."

Sister Catherine smiled. "*I* didn't, Mother. But perhaps the Blessed Virgin has. Shall I go to him now?"

"Of course. Someone else can take over the work in the kitchen."

So Sister Catherine hurried off to the infirmary, where she found John waiting for her impatiently.

"Sister, I fell asleep during your story," he said. "Now—well, will you tell me the rest of it? *Please?*"

In spite of herself, Sister Catherine stared in amazement. Please! Why, old John was never known to use such a word! Moreover, the fever had left him, and he was looking remarkably well and untroubled. Could it really be possible that Our Lady's medal....

Quickly she found a chair and sat down beside the bed. "Of course I'll tell you the rest of the story," she said, smiling. "Just where were we?"

"At the part about the old priest in the dream, Sister. You were afraid of him, and ran away when he wanted to talk to you. But he said that some day you would seek him out."

"Yes. Well, I was eighteen when I had that dream, John, and for a long time afterwards I used to wonder about it. 'Who is that old priest?' I would ask myself. 'And why can't I put his face out of my mind?' "

John's eyes were eager. "Well, who was he, Sister? Someone you knew?"

Sister Catherine shook her head. "No, John. He was a total stranger to me. But four years later, when I was twenty-two...."

"Yes?"

"My father arranged for me to leave home to visit my brother Charles and his wife Madeleine in Paris. They owned a restaurant, and Father thought that if I could work there as a waitress and meet some interesting people, I'd forget all about wanting to be a religious."

"But you didn't."

"No, I was miserable in Paris. And I was so shy and awkward that I made a wretched waitress. So, after a few months, it was decided that I should leave the restaurant and go to school."

"School! When you were twenty-two years old?"

"Yes. You see, I hadn't been to school very much,

"IT WAS THE OLD PRIEST OF MY DREAM!"

living in the country, and I longed to be able to read and write well. Then, too, I felt that if I was a little smarter, it would be more likely that some convent would accept me."

Sister Catherine then went on to describe her life in Chatillon (a town not far from Paris), where her brother Hubert and his wife Jane had a boarding school for girls. Here she had stayed for nearly a year, doing her best to learn all she could and trying to adapt herself to her new circumstances. But it had been very hard. The girls at school were so much younger than herself—twelve and fourteen years old —and some of them were inclined to look down on a young woman from the country who was so slow with books.

"I got so discouraged, John! Then one day Hubert's wife took me to visit the local hospital. It was run by the Daughters of Charity, and as we waited in the parlor for one of the Sisters to come...."

"Yes?"

"I noticed a certain picture on the wall. Oh, John! Guess what!"

"What, Sister?"

"It was the old priest of my dream! And he was Saint Vincent de Paul, the founder of the Daughters of Charity! Then as I looked at the picture, I heard those same strange words again: 'My child, you avoid me just now, but a day will come when you will seek me out. God expects something from you. Don't forget that.' "

OLD JOHN FINALLY AGREES
TO WEAR THE MEDAL

CHAPTER 11

S JOHN listened to the rest of the story
—how twenty-three-year-old Zoe Catherine Labouré, with the help of her
brother Hubert and his wife Jane, had
finally prevailed upon her father to let
her enter the Daughters of Charity, he felt a welling-
up of sympathy within himself such as he had not
experienced in many years. What a touching story!
To think that a twelve-year-old girl should have so
much love for God that she could spend almost another twelve years in preparing herself by prayer
and suffering to do what she felt was His Will for
her!

"Sister...." he began, then fell silent. What was
the use of asking questions? To love God as Sister
Catherine loved Him was surely a grace given to few
people. For men and women like himself who had
cheated, cursed, lied, stolen....

Sister Catherine seemed to read these thoughts.
"John, the good God loves each one of us—oh, so
much!—no matter what we have done to offend
Him."

"But I don't see...."

49

"Listen, John. What would you like most in the whole world?"

"I? Why, I...."

"You'd like to be happy, wouldn't you? Really and truly happy?"

"Y-yes."

"And you think that's impossible!"

"Oh, not for you, Sister. You're naturally kind and good. But for me...."

Sister Catherine leaned forward earnestly. "John, it's true that I've been given far more graces than you to help me to be happy. But isn't that because I've spent almost my whole life in asking for them?"

"Well...."

"Now tell me this. Do you love God? Really and truly?"

John shifted uneasily. "No, Sister. I'm afraid I don't."

"Well, have you ever asked Him to *help* you to love Him?"

"No."

"And why not?"

"I ... I guess I just never thought about it."

Suddenly Sister Catherine began to talk so naturally and confidently about God's desire to be loved, even by the most sinful and discouraged of souls, that John was impressed in spite of himself. How perfectly sure she seemed of the things she was saying! That people were meant to be happy, even in this world; that the only way to achieve this was to love God and say "yes" to what He wanted; to do one's duties faithfully, without complaint, and to get others to do the same. Even more. That sadness and discontent existed in the world chiefly because people were not *prepared* to be happy. They had never made an effort to know God, so that they might love and serve Him properly. Instead, they tried to know and love *things*—only to be disappointed at their emptiness. Yet anyone, no matter how poor or sinful, could prepare for real happiness and peace of mind. A fervent and continued prayer to know and love God, so that one might serve Him properly, was always answered. Then one had arrived, so to speak, at the threshold of joy.

John listened in silence, an expression of wonder on his face. "But I can't believe that happiness is that simple!" he said at last. "And I never thought that we could . . . well, *work* for it!"

Sister Catherine smiled. "It is, John! And we *can* work for it. But there's one more thing."

"What?"

The young nun slipped her hand into her pocket and drew out a Miraculous Medal. Here, she announced, was a likeness of a human creature who had loved God more than anyone else could ever love Him. And even in the midst of bitter trials and sufferings, she had been happy in a way that one can scarcely imagine.

"John, if you want to learn how to love God a good deal, and so to be happy in His service, why not ask the Blessed Virgin to help you? Why not wear this little medal around your neck?"

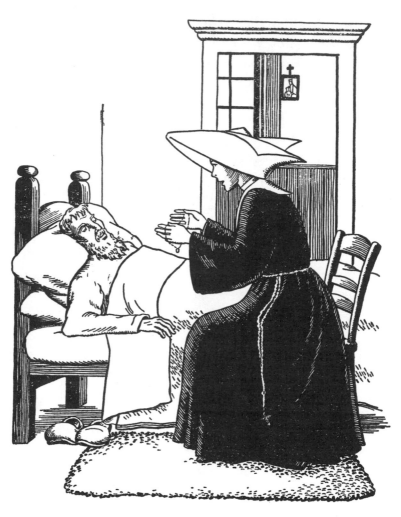

"JOHN, WHY NOT WEAR THIS LITTLE MEDAL?"

"B-but. . . ."

"I promise you one thing. If you do wear Our Lady's medal, and say that little prayer every day: *O Mary, conceived without sin, pray for us who have recourse to thee,* wonderful things are going to happen."

John smiled, a bit wryly. "I still can't believe that God is much concerned with me, Sister—whether I'm happy or not. But to please you—because after all *you* have been good to me—better than anyone else around here. . . ."

"You'll wear the medal?"

"Yes."

"And say the prayer, too?"

"Well. . . ."

"Please, John! That's very important!"

"All right. I'll say the prayer, too."

"Every day?"

"Every day."

THE GRACES PEOPLE FORGET
TO ASK FOR

CHAPTER 12

ATURALLY there was great astonishment at Enghien when it was discovered that old John had consented to wear a Miraculous Medal around his neck. Father Aladel was as surprised as anyone, and lost no time in questioning Sister Catherine about it.

"Sister, you don't really think that old man is going to be converted, do you?" he asked eagerly.

Sister Catherine hesitated. "I really couldn't say, Father. All I know is that I've put his case in Our Lady's hands. *She'll* look after him."

The priest looked closely at the young nun before him. "I think there's more to it than that, though. Come, now—isn't there?"

Sister Catherine lowered her eyes. "Well...."

"You've been praying for him constantly, haven't you? Especially at Mass?"

"Well ... yes, Father."

"And you've been making sacrifices, too?"

"Y-yes."

For a moment Father Aladel was silent. Long ago he had discovered what Sister Catherine's sacrifices were. Never complaining about the hardships

54

of working in a hot kitchen; never asking for privileges; kneeling for private prayer in the chapel when it would have been quite in order to sit; fasting on various days....

"It certainly would be wonderful if old John were converted," he observed finally. Then, after a moment: "Sister, tell me this. Does the Blessed Virgin ever appear to you these days?"

Sister Catherine shook her head. "No, Father. I've never seen her since I left the Motherhouse. But don't you remember that she told me this, just before I received the habit: 'My child, you will not see me any longer, although you will hear my voice in your meditations'?"

Father Aladel nodded thoughtfully. "Yes, I remember. But I was just wondering...."

"No, Father. She never comes any more. But I do hear her speaking to me at certain times."

"And what does she say?"

Once again Sister Catherine hesitated. How could she put into words what Our Lady had told her? That within less than forty years troubles of all kinds would come to France? Revolution, bloodshed, martyrdom for young and old? That even now, despite the many graces being won for them through devotion to the Miraculous Medal, there were several among the Daughters of Charity and the Priests of the Mission—the two religious families which Saint Vincent de Paul had founded—who were not faithful to their duties? Who spent only a little time in prayer and spiritual reading? Who preferred the

"NO, FATHER. SHE NEVER COMES ANY MORE."

company of rich and important people to that of the poor and sick?

Yet Father Aladel was her confessor, sent by God to be her spiritual guide, and so Sister Catherine did her best to recall for him Our Lady's words. But when she had finished speaking and was about to lapse into silence, a sudden thought struck her.

"Father, do you remember when the Blessed Virgin came to me the second time at the Motherhouse, some of the rings on her fingers were bright and sparkling while others gave forth no light at all?"

The priest nodded. "Yes, Sister. I remember. You told me then that the rings without any light represented the graces for which we forget to ask."

"That's right. Oh, how I wish you could get people to understand this—*really* understand it!"

"I? But how can I do anything?"

"Why, in your sermons, Father. Our Lady can give so many wonderful things, if only people will ask her for them. But they ask for so many ... well, *unimportant* things instead! Can't you say something about this when you talk to people?"

For a moment the priest was silent. He had often thought about this very matter, and had made several efforts to discover just what the graces were for which people—himself included—never thought to pray. But it had not been easy. Undoubtedly there were so many! For instance, the grace of a cheerful disposition. How many people ever thought to ask the Blessed Virgin for this? Or for the grace to recognize and accept the trials of everyday life as blessings from God? Or to love all men as brothers, and to wish them well? Or to be contented with one's state in life? Or to understand and appreciate the Holy Sacrifice of the Mass?

"Well, what *are* the graces for which we forget to pray?" he asked. "And how would you explain things in a sermon if you were in my place?"

For a moment Sister Catherine did not reply. Then a soft light crept into her eyes. "Why not put it this way, Father? Tell people to ask the Blessed Virgin for the grace to love God as she did when she was their age."

At these words, so simply spoken, a wave of admiration swept through the priest's heart. Here, surely, was a request that only a few people would ever think of making. Yet certainly it covered everything. Indeed, it was nothing short of a perfect act of love. Why, if one offered this little prayer frequently, while being faithful to the duties of one's state in life, there was no reason to be afraid of anything! Not even of sudden death. For a perfect act of love could bring even the most ordinary soul straight to heaven.

OLD JOHN DECIDES TO
GO TO CONFESSION

CHAPTER 13

URING the months that followed, Father Aladel's sermons were chiefly concerned with this suggestion of Sister Catherine's. Over and over again he described how Our Lady had appeared at the Motherhouse of the Daughters of Charity, her fingers covered with rings that glistened like the sun, while other rings gave forth no light at all. Repeatedly he urged his listeners to ask the Blessed Virgin for *important* things when they prayed to her.

"Health, success in business, a comfortable home—these are all good in themselves," he admitted. "But what a pity to be content with them! Oh, my friends! Why not ask the Blessed Virgin for the grace to love God as she loved Him when she was our age? That prayer surely covers everything!"

So earnestly did he speak that soon devotion to the Miraculous Medal was becoming stronger than ever. By the end of 1834—two years after the first medals had appeared—one Paris factory reported that it alone had sold two million gold and silver medals, and eighteen million brass ones. Twelve other factories had sold more than a million each, while in the city of Lyons four storekeepers had dispatched a total of thirty million medals to customers from all over the world.

Sister Catherine was delighted. Millions of people were now wearing Our Lady's medal? Thousands of cures and other blessings were being attributed to her intercession? How wonderful! Yet of all the accounts of favors received, one which occurred at Enghien brought Sister Catherine a special happiness. For without the slightest warning, old John announced one day that he wanted to go to confession!

"Sister, I just won't have any peace until I do," he confided. "Do you suppose I could see the chaplain right away?"

Sister Catherine stared in amazement. "You don't mean...."

"Yes, Sister. I do mean it. For weeks now I haven't been able to sleep at night. I keep seeing myself as God must see me—black with sin—and I'm afraid to close my eyes. I tell you, if it weren't for that little prayer that you made me promise to say—"

"O Mary, conceived without sin, pray for us who have recourse to thee?"

"Yes. If it weren't for that, I'd be scared to death!"

Grateful tears glistened in Sister Catherine's eyes. How truly John spoke! The prayer on the front of the Miraculous Medal did have a wonderful power to

MILLIONS OF MEDALS HAD BEEN SOLD.

comfort and encourage souls. A person had only to say it, slowly and devoutly, to experience its extraordinary effect. Thus, even this poor old man before her who had caused everyone so much trouble. . . .

"John, you've made me very happy," she declared, scarcely able to conceal her excitement. "But maybe we'd better not talk any more just now. After all, you do want to see the chaplain, don't you?"

John nodded. "Yes. But there's something else, too, Sister."

"What?"

"If . . . if I do make a good confession. . . ."

Sister Catherine stretched out her hand in reassurance. "Of course you'll make a good confession, John. There isn't the slightest doubt about it."

"I hope not, Sister. But once I have, there's something I'd like to do as a . . . a kind of thanksgiving. That is, if you think it would be all right."

Sister Catherine leaned forward earnestly. What a day of miracles this was!

"Yes, John? What is it?"

"I'd like to try to get the men here who haven't much interest in the medal to wear it around their necks. You know, there are still quite a few who think it's only for women and girls. But maybe they'd listen to me, remembering how I used to say the same thing. . . ."

Suddenly Sister Catherine's happiness was full to overflowing. The Miraculous Medal! How truly it was named! How wonderfully the Blessed Virgin rewarded those who wore it in her honor! And yet, was it wise to show much astonishment at John's unexpected suggestion? Might it not make him feel a little awkward and self-conscious, and so spoil everything?

"John, I think your idea is a splendid one," she declared, in as matter-of-fact a voice as she could manage. "I'm quite sure Our Lady thinks so, too." Then, after a moment: "But what about the chaplain? Shall I go and get him for you?"

The old man hesitated, then nodded slowly and squared his shoulders. "Yes, Sister. Go and get him. And ... and please pray for me!"

THE CHILDREN OF MARY

CHAPTER 14

Y THE grace of God and with the help of the Blessed Virgin, John did make a good confession. Then, as he had promised, he did all that he could to promote devotion to the Miraculous Medal among the other old men at Enghien. And so well did he succeed that finally there was not one who was not wearing it about his neck.

Noting this, many people were convinced that it was Sister Catherine to whom Our Lady had appeared.

"Who else could it be?" they asked one another earnestly. "Surely only someone who has seen the Blessed Virgin could make such an obstinate old sinner as John wear her medal—and then get his friends to do the same!"

But as the weeks passed and Sister Catherine only laughed at such stories—calmly busying herself with her usual kitchen duties—there began to be doubts. Yes, Sister Catherine Labouré was holy. And kind and sympathetic. But after all, so were many of the other Sisters. And when it was presently announced that Sister Catherine was to leave her work in the kitchen for duties in the laundry and linen room, all seemed clear. If she had been the one to whom Our Lady had appeared, she would surely have been given a far more important work to do than this.

"It's someone else who saw the Blessed Virgin," was the general opinion. "Probably Sister Claire."

"That's right. Or Sister Martha."

"Or Sister Pauline."

Of course Father Aladel took no part in any such discussion. Had he not faithfully promised Sister Catherine to respect her confidence? Then again, most of their talks about the apparitions had taken place at the time of confession, so that it was utterly impossible for him to discuss details with anyone. Yet his interest in Sister Catherine never wavered, and he looked forward to each of his trips from Paris to Enghien with eager expectation. Perhaps the Blessed Virgin had come to Sister Catherine again! Perhaps she had given her a special message for him!

In the fall of the year 1836—some six years after the apparitions at the Motherhouse—Sister Catherine did have a heavenly message for her confessor.

"I didn't see the Blessed Virgin, Father, but I heard her voice while I was praying in the chapel," she told him excitedly. "And she has another work for you to do."

The priest's heart beat fast. "What kind of work, Sister?"

"She wants you to found a society for young girls, Father—a spiritual society to be called 'The Children of Mary.'"

"IT'S SISTER MARTHA WHO SAW OUR LADY...."

Gone were the days when Father Aladel would have questioned the source of such a command, although the thought did flash across his mind that there were already several societies for girls and women dedicated to the Blessed Virgin. Therefore, what was the need for another?

"Sister, how do I go about founding the Children of Mary?" he asked eagerly.

Sister Catherine lost no time in explaining matters. The new group was to be made up of young girls being cared for in the schools and orphanages of the Daughters of Charity. And the requirements for membership were to be very simple. The girls were to wear Our Lady's medal day and night. They were to meet regularly to say the Rosary, the Litany of Loreto, the *Memorare* and other prayers in honor of the Blessed Virgin. There were to be processions and various devotions, especially in May.

"In other words, Father, you're to train these little ones to have a great and trusting love for the Blessed Virgin," explained Sister Catherine. "In that way, they'll grow up to think of her as their best friend."

Father Aladel humbly promised to do what he could, and on December 8 of that same year—1836 —received the first members of the new society. And with a truly grateful heart, for by now he was beginning to realize just why the Blessed Virgin had asked that such a group be formed.

"In France, all the other societies existing in her honor are made up of those with plenty of this world's goods," he reflected. "Very little has ever been done to bring the poor together in her name. But now—oh, how splendid that we have the Children of Mary!"

Sister Catherine agreed. "That's right, Father. When our little ones leave us to go to work in the shops and factories, they'll stand a much better chance of leading good lives—consecrated as they are to the Blessed Virgin, and trained to call upon her in all their trials and troubles."

OUR LADY CONVERTS
AN ANTI-CATHOLIC JEW

CHAPTER 15

OON Father Aladel was doing everything possible to focus public attention on the Children of Mary. But as he generally spoke with Sister Catherine only in the confessional (he was accustomed to come regularly from Paris to Enghien to look after the spiritual needs of the Sisters), no one suspected that she had any special part to play in the new movement. Yet the whole affair was very close to her heart.

"Father, why couldn't boys as well as girls be members of the Children of Mary?" she asked one day. "I've been praying about this for a long time, and I'm sure it's what the Blessed Virgin wants."

The priest hesitated. *"Boys,* Sister?"

"Yes, the little boys taught by the Daughters of Charity and the older boys taught by your own community—the Priests of the Mission."

For a moment Father Aladel was thoughtful. For over three centuries the Jesuit Fathers had been enrolling their students in a society whose chief purpose was to honor the Mother of God. This was *La Prima Primaria,* established by Pope Gregory the Thirteenth in 1534. Now, how splendid if there might be something similar for the young boys who were being cared for by the Daughters of Charity and for those who were students of the Priests of the Mission! Then if devotion to the Miraculous Medal could also be worked in in some way, . . .

"Sister, you're right," he declared finally. "There's no reason why boys of all ages shouldn't be members of the Children of Mary. Nor why both boys and girls shouldn't have a special blessing from the Holy Father, with the chance to gain many indulgences on Our Lady's feast days."

But how to go about making this possible? For months Father Aladel prayed and thought about the idea. His friend and fellow-religious, Father Etienne, did the same. And in the end it was decided that one of them ought to go to Rome to lay the matter before the Holy Father. Surely the Children of Mary could be affiliated in some way with *La Prima Primaria*, the society which the Jesuit Fathers had founded three hundred years before, and which was so richly blessed with indulgences?

But before any definite plans could be made, something wonderful happened. Early in 1842 news reached Paris of the extraordinary conversion in Rome of a wealthy young Jew named Alphonse Ratisbonne. And since the event was definitely connected with the Miraculous Medal, excitement was at fever pitch among the two families of Saint Vincent de Paul.

"The young man saw Our Lady!" the Daughters

of Charity told one another eagerly. "She showed herself to him just as she appears on the medal!"

The Priests of the Mission were equally excited. "Yes, in spite of the fact that he didn't believe in her, and had no use for the medal," they said.

Sister Catherine was delighted. Someone else had seen the Blessed Virgin? How splendid! And what a joy it would be to have a few words with this young man! Yet how could an obscure nun dare to ask for such a favor without betraying her own most precious secret?

In the end Sister Catherine contented herself with hearing the details of Alphonse Ratisbonne's conversion from Father Aladel. She discovered that the young man in question, a native of Strasburg and soon to be married, had been traveling through Italy on his way to the Holy Land. But he had purposely avoided going to Rome. His brother, Theodore, had been converted to the Faith, and Alphonse had never ceased to resent it, especially since conversion had been followed by ordination to the priesthood. Through the years he had built up a strong prejudice against all things Christian. In fact, the very sight of a Catholic church filled him with the bitterest aversion. Yet at the last moment he had changed his mind and gone to Rome, where he had by chance made the acquaintance of Count Theodore de Bussière, an ardent convert.

"The Count was deeply devoted to the Miraculous Medal," Father Aladel explained. "And after a great deal of persuasion, he prevailed upon young

Alphonse to wear it about his neck. What's more, he even got him to postpone his trip to Jerusalem and to go about with him to various churches in Rome. And he also got him to copy out the *Memorare* in his own handwriting and to promise to say it morning and night."

Sister Catherine's eyes shone. "But these were almost miracles in themselves!" she declared, remembering her own struggles to convert old John. "And if the young man was a Jew, Father—not even baptized. . . ."

The priest nodded. "He was just about as prejudiced as Saul of Tarsus against the Christian faith, Sister. In fact, several times he was on the point of breaking off his friendship with the Count because the Count was always wanting to talk to him about religion. But on January 20, the Feast of Saints Fabian and Sebastian. . . ."

"Yes?"

"He consented to go with his new friend to one more church—that of St. Andrea delle Fratte. After that, he would be off for the Holy Land."

With a fast-beating heart Sister Catherine heard the remaining details: How, restless and impatient, Alphonse Ratisbonne had nevertheless agreed to remain in church while Count de Bussière made a hurried trip to the adjoining monastery to inquire about the funeral of the Marquis de la Ferronnays (one of his best friends) which was to be held the next day; how presently he had wandered about the church, watching the preparations for the funeral, finally coming to a stop before a side chapel dedicated to Saint Michael the Archangel. Here, without the slightest warning, Our Lady had appeared to him, standing upon the altar—tall, bright, majestic, full of sweetness—with heavenly rays streaming from her outstretched hands. But so dazzlingly beautiful had she been that the astonished young Jew had not been able to gaze steadfastly upon her. Three times he had tried, but after his first flashing look he could lift his eyes no higher than her hands, blazing with unearthly light.

For a moment Sister Catherine could not speak. Then she leaned forward eagerly. "What ... what did Our Lady say to the young man, Father?" she whispered.

The priest shook his head. "Nothing."

"*Nothing!*"

"No. She just looked at him, indicated that he should kneel, and in an instant made him understand the true state of his soul. Then after a little while she disappeared."

"What about the Count?"

"He was gone only a few minutes, and when he first came back to the church he couldn't find his young friend at all. He thought he'd grown tired of waiting, and was going outside to look for him. Then suddenly he spied him, *kneeling* in the chapel of Saint Michael with tears streaming down his face, clutching the Miraculous Medal about his neck."

"Wasn't he terribly surprised, Father?"

HE COULD LIFT HIS EYES NO HIGHER THAN HER HANDS.

"Surprised? Sister, he was dumbfounded! Especially when Alphonse would tell him nothing of what had happened, only begged to be taken to a priest."

"Of course the Count took him to one?"

"Yes, to a very holy Jesuit. And soon the whole story was out. Our Lady, as she appears on the medal, had shown herself to Alphonse Ratisbonne, and now nothing would do but that he should be baptized and spend the rest of his life in telling people about her—especially about the graces that she has in store for those who ask her help."

Sister Catherine's joy knew no bounds. What a wonderful story! Surely now there would be more devotion than ever to the Miraculous Medal—not only in France and Italy but in every part of the world!

THE RAYS

CHAPTER 16

OR the rest of the day Sister Catherine could think of nothing but the miracle which had taken place in the far-away church of St. Andrea delle Fratte on January 20. Why, in many ways it was as wonderful and mysterious as the conversion of Saint Paul himself! Then presently there was fresh cause to marvel, for word reached Paris that Alphonse Ratisbonne was not going to be just another Catholic. No, he was going to be a priest. He felt quite sure that this was God's Will for him, and so he had broken off his marriage engagement and was about to enter a seminary. Perhaps some day he might even join his priest-brother Theodore and work for the conversion of the entire Jewish race.

As she reflected upon this surprising turn of events, Sister Catherine's thoughts kept turning to one special aspect of Our Lady's recent apparition:

At first Alphonse Ratisbonne had looked full upon her. But only for a moment. Her beauty and brightness had been too much to bear. Afterwards his glance could rise no higher than her hands. He had seen, just as Sister Catherine herself had seen twelve years before, the rays of glory flowing from

76

*those hands. And he, too, had been allowed to under-
stand that these were more than a mysterious and
heavenly light. They were graces and blessings—
gifts beyond all price—ready to be had for the asking!*

"If only people everywhere could understand all
this!" Sister Catherine told herself longingly. "How
eager they would be to kneel before Our Lady's
picture or statue and ask for a share of the good
things she longs to give!"

Presently more details were forthcoming concerning the Ratisbonne conversion, including the young
man's personal account of what had happened.
Sister Catherine read and pondered everything, especially the part concerning the light from Our
Lady's hands.

"I cannot give an idea in words," declared the
twenty-eight-year-old convert, "of the mercy and
generosity I felt to be expressed in those hands. It
was not only rays of light that I saw escaping from
them. Words fail to give an idea of the wonderful
gifts that flow from the hands of Our Mother! The
mercy, the tenderness and the wealth of heaven es-
cape in torrents on the souls whom Mary protects."

Father Aladel was just as impressed as Sister
Catherine with the reference to Our Lady's hands
as the source of all grace for suffering man-
kind. Over and over again he stressed this point in
his sermons, so that gradually people began to see
the picture on the Miraculous Medal in a new light.
Those heavenly rays streaming earthwards in a

blaze of glory—they were not just a whim of the artist who had designed the medal. No, indeed. They had a real and important meaning.

"Ask! Ask! Ask!" the priest urged his listeners, young and old. "There's nothing that the Blessed Virgin can't obtain for you if you have trust and confidence." Then, as an afterthought: "But don't forget the most important thing of all—the grace to love God as she loved Him when she lived on earth."

Sister Catherine did not hear many of Father Aladel's sermons, since he did not often preach at Enghien. But she well knew of his efforts to promote a love of Our Lady, and her heart swelled with joy. If only more priests could be found to speak with similar devotion! If only people everywhere could understand about Our Lady's hands!

"Surely this nineteenth century is 'The Age of Mary,'" she reflected. "God seems to want people to come to Him through His Mother as never before."

The Age of Mary! As the years passed, Sister Catherine became more and more convinced that this era had arrived. So many things continued to happen which proved it! For instance, on September 19, 1846, near the obscure French village of La Salette, the Blessed Virgin had appeared once again—this time to two peasant children, fourteen-year-old Melanie Mathieu and eleven-year-old Maximin Giraud— with the message that people must turn away from sin and do penance, otherwise great sorrow would come upon the world. In particular, they must keep Sundays holy and refrain from bad language. Then,

"IT IS THE AGE OF MARY," THOUGHT SISTER CATHERINE.

in the year 1847, the Association of the Children of Mary had been canonically established by Pope Pius the Ninth and granted all the privileges of *La Prima Primaria.*

Even more. In 1850 the Holy Father had extended membership in the Children of Mary to the young boys cared for by the Daughters of Charity and to the older ones studying under the Priests of the Mission. Then in 1854 the doctrine of the Immaculate Conception had been solemnly proclaimed as an Article of Faith, while in 1858 there had been still further apparitions of the Blessed Virgin—this time to Bernadette Soubirous, a young girl living at Lourdes, a town near the Spanish-French border.

"It *is* the Age of Mary," Sister Catherine assured herself happily.

Yet even as she rejoiced, her heart told her that this was only the beginning of the Blessed Virgin's earthly mission in modern times. Yes, the nineteenth century was witnessing her power for good in an extraordinary way. But surely within the next hundred years Our Lady would be still more in evidence as she brought untold millions to a greater knowledge and love of her Son?

"The twentieth century!" thought Sister Catherine. "That will be the time when the Blessed Mother will really speak to souls—at her shrines, in her apparitions, yes—and through the Miraculous Medal, too!"

"THE STREETS WILL
RUN WITH BLOOD"

CHAPTER 17

HEN Sister Catherine first came to Enghien, she had been told to work in the
kitchen. After that, there had been duties in the linen room and laundry. But
finally came her permanent assignment.
She was to be in charge of the fifty old men who had
no other home than that provided for them by the
Daughters of Charity.

How Sister Catherine loved this new work! She
had a genuine gift for nursing, and when she could
make some old man a little more comfortable, or
prove to him that even though he was poor and sick
and feeble he could still be of use to others by offering his pains for them, her heart filled with joy. In
one sense, she had given up everything to work
among God's poor—human love, children, a home of
her own. Yet how generously she was being rewarded, even in this world! How good to be loved
and needed by fifty souls, each of whom, through
Baptism, represented Christ Himself!

"Lord, thank You for bringing me here!" she
often prayed. "And please help me to work for You
as perfectly as possible!"

81

HOW GOOD TO BE LOVED AND NEEDED BY THE POOR!

Time passed, uneventfully. Then on April 25, 1865, when she was fifty-nine years old, a trial which she had been dreading for a long time overtook Sister Catherine. Father Aladel, her trusted friend and confessor, fell ill and died! Now there was no one in the whole world to whom she could speak freely about Our Lady's apparitions or the promotion of the Miraculous Medal. For had she not been told by Our Lady herself, some thirty-five years before, to discuss these matters only with the one who had charge of her soul?

"Perhaps now the Blessed Virgin will tell me to confide in some other priest," she thought hopefully. "Or maybe in one of the Sisters."

But although Sister Catherine waited and prayed, there was no heavenly message to this effect. Not even five years later, when France was involved in the misery of the Franco-Prussian war, did Our Lady speak.

Sister Catherine's heart was heavy. The year 1870—what a dreadful time it was, with so much suffering and bloodshed! Nor were matters improved with the arrival of 1871, for then a group of vicious men made a sudden attempt to overthrow the government and stamp out all religion. Once again Paris was under siege, and the streets of the city filled with dead and wounded. Priests and nuns were murdered in cold blood, churches desecrated, and one religious community after another forced to close its doors.

Amid the scenes of terror about her, Sister Catherine often recalled the sorrowful words she had heard on the occasion of Our Lady's first visit on that far-away night of July 18, 1830:

"My child, the times are evil. Misfortunes are about to overwhelm France ... the whole world will be convulsed by all sorts of calamities ... there will be victims in religious communities ... the Archbishop will die ... the Cross will be despised and trodden under foot; the side of Our Lord will be pierced anew; the streets will run with blood; the whole world will be in sorrow...."

But of course there were other and more comforting words to remember, too:

"Come to the foot of the altar. There graces will be showered upon you and all who ask for them, whatever their rank or position. A moment will come when the danger will be great. People will think that all is lost. I shall be with you then. Do not lose confidence. You will feel that I am present, and that God and Saint Vincent are protecting the two communities. Trust, and do not be discouraged...."

Naturally the Superiors of the Daughters of Charity were beside themselves with anxiety. Should the community also take flight? Or should it remain to provide for the safety of the orphans and the old folks in its care?

In the end it was decided that the Sisters should stay at their posts and use their convents as hospitals (as they had done all during the Franco-Prussian

War) for the sake of the wounded of both sides. Surely even the godless men behind the Revolution could not object to that.

For several weeks, with shells bursting all around them and their house a haven for anyone in need, the Sisters at Enghien waited and prayed. Would the Christian forces be able to overcome the rebels, or was the Revolution going to succeed? If so, would they be allowed to remain where they were, or would they also be thrown into prison and sentenced to die at the hands of the mob?

Despite the constant danger, Sister Catherine's courage did not falter. "The Blessed Virgin will look after us," she told her fellow-religious. "After all, aren't we wearing her medal and getting others to do the same?"

Then without warning came the verdict which everyone had feared. The Sisters must leave Enghien at once, declared the rebels. Their convent? It would be turned into a fortress. In a week, two weeks, boasted these ruthless men who had taken over the government, God would be driven from Paris. And after that, from all of France.

A NEW REQUEST FROM OUR LADY

CHAPTER 18

N ACCORDANCE with orders, the Sisters left Enghien on April 30, 1871—some to seek safety in Toulouse, others for towns not so far away. Thus, the community was broken up. However, the time of their exile was to be short, and in less than four weeks there was good news. The Revolution was over! Loyal French troops had defeated the rebels in Paris and freed the city from its reign of terror. Of course there had been a terrific price to pay. Thousands of innocent people had lost their lives, including the Archbishop of Paris and many priests and nuns. But the danger was over now. At any time the Sisters might return in safety to their Motherhouse. And to the convent at Enghien, too.

"Didn't I tell you that Our Lady of the Miraculous Medal would look after us?" cried Sister Catherine eagerly. "Why, we'll be back home while it's still May—*her* month!"

The Sisters looked at one another, relief and joy mingled with astonishment. Yes, Sister Catherine had said that everything would be all right; that they

"DIDN'T I TELL YOU THAT OUR LADY WOULD LOOK AFTER US?"

would even crown Our Lady's statue in May as they had always done. But somehow no one had paid much attention to her during the terror and confusion of those last horrible days in the city. . . .

"Yes, Sister, you did say just that," agreed the Superior. "And when we get back, we'll certainly have a real celebration in honor of Our Lady of the Miraculous Medal. Something that will show her just how much we appreciate all she's done for us."

So it came to pass. At the first possible moment a solemn Mass of Thanksgiving was offered in every house of the Daughters of Charity, and devotion to the Miraculous Medal urged upon all as never before. But even as Sister Catherine rejoiced with the rest of the community that peace had finally come to France, a new anxiey was tugging at her heart. She had received another message from heaven! And since Father Aladel was dead, there was no one now with whom to share it!

"Our Lady wants a statue made," she told herself uneasily. "One that will show her as she appeared on her second visit, holding a golden globe in her hands with a little cross on top. But . . . but how can *I* do anything about it?"

Poor Sister Catherine! She did have a problem. For how could she say even one word about the statue without revealing the precious secret which she had kept for more than forty years—namely, that she was the one to whom Our Lady had appeared in 1830, and that ever since she had been privileged to hear her voice from time to time while at prayer in the chapel? That of all the people living in the world, she was the one most directly concerned with devotion to the Miraculous Medal?

"If only Father Aladel were here!" she kept thinking, distressed beyond words at her inability to do anything. "Then I could tell him privately what Our Lady wants, and he could have the statue made without any trouble. But this way...."

For weeks Sister Catherine prayed and thought about the matter. As usual she had not seen the Blessed Virgin, but she had heard her voice while at prayer. And there was no mistaking the fact that the heavenly one was eager that people should have a new image of herself. Not as she was shown on the medal, with rays of glory streaming from her hands, but as she had appeared on November 27, 1830, when holding the golden globe—the world—to her heart, then offering it to God and interceding for its sins.

"Dearest Mother, won't you please tell me what to do?" asked Sister Catherine earnestly.

But the months passed, and then the years, and her prayer went unanswered. There was only the occasional miracle of the Blessed Virgin's voice—motherly, kind, sympathetic—patiently repeating her request that the statue be made.

By the year 1876 the strain of not being able to obey Our Lady's wishes had become so great that Sister Catherine's health began to fail. No longer was she able to spend the whole day with her beloved charges—the fifty old men who made their home at Enghien. Even another work which had always been more of recreation than of labor—the care of the poultry yard—became too much for her.

"Sister Catherine's not herself at all," the Sisters told one another anxiously. "What do you suppose is wrong?"

There were several earnest consultations. "Maybe she's just getting old," suggested someone finally. "After all, she's seventy now. That, with her rheumatism. . . ."

"But she looks and acts so worried! Just as though something terrible were on her mind! In all the years we've known her, she's never been like that."

The Superior agreed. "We'll have the doctor look at her again," she promised. "Perhaps he could give her a different medicine. Or maybe extra treatments for her rheumatism would help."

Of course Sister Catherine appreciated the interest being taken in her, but she felt that it was all quite useless. Her days on earth were about over. She would never live to see the year 1877. And . . . and how terrible to die without having done what Our Lady had asked of her!

"Perhaps after all it wouldn't hurt to talk to someone about the statue," she ventured to think one day. "Maybe to Father Chinchon. He's a very holy man. Surely he'd know what to do."

In a moment the decision was made. "Yes, that's it," Sister Catherine told herself, much relieved. "I'll go to see Father Chinchon right away and tell him everything."

A DISAPPOINTING TRIP

CHAPTER 19

ATURALLY the Mother Superior was not a little concerned when Sister Catherine asked permission to go to see Father Chinchon. For one who was feeble and suffering such pain, the jolting trip by carriage to Saint Lazare (the Paris headquarters of the Priests of the Mission) would surely be too much.

"Why not wait until Father Chinchon comes here?" she suggested kindly. "After all, since he's our confessor...."

But Sister Catherine did not even seem to hear. "There's something I must ask Father right away," she insisted. "Please let me go, Mother!"

Against her better judgment, the Mother Superior finally gave permission, and presently Sister Catherine and a companion were on their way to Saint Lazare. But when they reached their destination, they discovered that Father Chinchon was not at home. He had just been transferred to a new post, and another and much younger priest appointed confessor for the Sisters at Enghien.

"But I *must* see Father Chinchon!" cried Sister Catherine when the Superior of the Priests of the Mission came into the parlor. "Father, couldn't you

91

"PLEASE LET ME GO, MOTHER!"

have him brought back? It's . . . it's so important!"

The Superior looked closely at his visitor. What a fine religious she was! What wonders she had accomplished with the old men at Enghien! But surely right now she was acting just a trifle childish?

"Sister, if you want to go to confession, there are plenty of other priests here to help you," he said cheerfully. "Or maybe you could tell me what's the trouble. Now, suppose you sit down—"

But Sister Catherine shook her head, while tears of disappointment clouded her eyes. "N-no. I can't talk to anyone but Father Chinchon."

"But I've told you he's not here, Sister. He's away on very important business."

Sister Catherine nodded. "I know, Father. But you're the Superior. You could have him come home. Won't you? *Please?*"

The priest made a valiant effort to control his impatience. What was the matter with this old Sister? Didn't she realize that it was most unreasonable to expect to see a busy missionary who was many miles from Paris?

"I'm sorry," he repeated, a trifle stiffly. "I couldn't very well do that, Sister."

As the minutes passed, the dreadful truth began to dawn upon Sister Catherine. The trip to Saint Lazare had been a failure! No matter how much she argued and pleaded, she was not going to be able to see Father Chinchon!

Scarcely able to control her disappointment, she finally motioned to her companion that it was time to go. But all the way back to Enghien, she wept through fatigue and discouragement. What was to be done now? She simply had to speak to someone about the statue! It was almost summer of the year 1876, and something told her that she had only a few months more to live. Yet how could she calmly face the thought of death without first having done everything possible to fulfill Our Lady's request?

Naturally Sister Catherine's companion was beside herself with anxiety. "Sister, what *is* the trouble?" she kept demanding. "I'd so like to help you if I could!"

With a great effort Sister Catherine managed a reassuring smile. "N-nothing's the trouble," she declared. "I'm just a little tired, that's all."

"But it must be more than that, Sister! Why, I've never seen you so upset before! Won't you please tell me what's the matter?"

Slowly Sister Catherine shook her head. Somehow she was beginning to feel that the Mother Superior was the only one in whom she ought to confide. What did it matter that she would have to tell her everything, including the fact that she—Sister Catherine Labouré—was actually the privileged Sister of the Miraculous Medal? That possibly, when the whole story was out, the Mother Superior might not even believe it?

"It's the only thing to do," she told herself silently. "But just to make sure, I'll pray about things a little more. Then, if Our Lady says 'yes', I'll go to see Reverend Mother in the morning."

SISTER CATHERINE BREAKS
HER LONG SILENCE

CHAPTER 20

S SOON as she reached Enghien, Sister Catherine went in search of the Mother Superior to ask if she might see her in the parlor at ten o'clock the next day.

"I think I'll have something to say to you then, Mother. But first I'm going to ask Our Lady about it at meditation."

The Superior looked closely at the old nun before her. What an odd statement!

"Why couldn't you tell me now?" she suggested kindly. "I have some free time."

But Sister Catherine shook her head. "Oh, no, Mother! I have to make sure of what I want to say. You see, it's been a secret for *such* a long time! Then again, maybe I'm not meant to say anything."

The Mother Superior smiled indulgently. "Very well, Sister. I'll be in the parlor at ten o'clock tomorrow if you want to talk to me."

With a sense of real relief, Sister Catherine took her departure. And when, at meditation the next morning, she heard Our Lady's voice giving permission to confide in the Mother Superior, she was a new person. How good to know that in a little while the responsibility for having the statue made would no longer be hers alone!

Long before the hour appointed she was in the parlor, her eyes shining with childlike eagerness.

"Mother, Our Lady said I could tell you everything!" she burst out happily as the Superior entered the room on the stroke of ten. "Nothing has to be a secret any longer. Oh, what a relief!"

Then, to the Superior's amazement, she launched into her story: How, almost since the first day of her arrival at the Motherhouse, she had been granted many favors. For instance, three times she had seen the heart of Saint Vincent de Paul floating in the air over the silver box in the chapel containing his relics; times without number Our Lord had appeared to her at Mass; then on the night of July 18, 1830, she had seen and talked with the Blessed Virgin for two hours, while on November 27 of that same year, and again in December, there had been the glorious visions of Our Lady of the Miraculous Medal.

The Superior listened in stupefied silence. "*You're* the Sister of the Miraculous Medal?" she burst out finally.

Sister Catherine hesitated, then lowered her eyes. "Yes, Mother," she said quietly. "And now Our Lady wants something else of me. And of you, too."

As the Superior continued to stare in awed amazement, Sister Catherine went on with her story. She had not seen Our Lady since the apparitions in the chapel of the Motherhouse, but hundreds of times while at prayer she had heard her voice. And now the heavenly one wanted a statue made, showing her as she had appeared when she had held the world in her hands—the golden ball surmounted with a small cross.

"You *will* see about the statue, Mother? That it's made right away and put on an altar at the place of the apparitions? It's so very important! And it's caused me so much worry!"

Slowly the Mother Superior began to recover her customary practicality. "But Sister!" she objected. "To speak of a statue now, after all these years—especially one that shows Our Lady in a different attitude to that in which she appears on the medal—won't it shake people's faith in the apparitions?"

Sister Catherine smiled. Oh, no, Mother!"

"But there'll be some who'll say that the medal ought to be changed!"

"No, leave the medal as it is."

"Without the globe in Our Lady's hands?"

"Without the globe."

Then, quite calmly, Sister Catherine went on to explain. The picture of the Blessed Virgin on the medal, showing her with rays of glory proceeding from her outstretched hands, was to help people to understand that, in God's plan, all graces and blessings are distributed through her. The statue, on the other hand, was to show her in another light—as constantly pleading for the world and begging God's mercy upon every sinner in it.

"Don't you see, Mother? Our Lady knows we're only children, and that our minds often get tired and wander. So she's seen to it that with the medal *and* the statue we may think about her in different ways. That's all."

Then she began to describe how the statue should be made. It ought to show Our Lady as of middle-age, smiling, motherly, yet not too joyful. Her dress and veil should be golden white—something like the color of the sky just before dawn—and beneath her feet she was to be crushing a green serpent with yellow spots.

"That's the Devil, Mother. Oh, how he's tried to keep me from having this statue made! You see, he can't bear the idea of thousands of people coming to pray before it... of their having still another way in which to think about the Blessed Virgin...."

On and on went Sister Catherine, describing the statue in still more detail. Then presently she sighed happily.

"That's all, Mother. There isn't any more to tell you."

The Superior scarcely knew what to say. To think that the little nun before her was the Sister of the Miraculous Medal! That for forty-six years she had kept all these wonderful things to herself—going about her duties in the kitchen, the laundry, the linen room, the poultry yard, among the old men, as though nothing unusual had ever happened to her! Then suddenly the Superior's amazement knew no bounds. The Angelus was beginning to ring!

"Sister, you've been talking to me for two solid hours!" she burst out. "And we've both been stand-

SHE BEGAN TO DESCRIBE THE STATUE.

ing the whole time! Why didn't you ask to sit down?"

Sister Catherine smiled. Time! What was that when one was talking about the Blessed Virgin?

"It's all right, Mother," she said hastily. "Don't worry. I'm just as surprised as you that the two hours went so quickly."

SISTER CATHERINE'S LAST REQUEST

CHAPTER 21

MAZED—and even disturbed—as she was by Sister Catherine's revelation, the Mother Superior nevertheless lost no time in procuring the services of a famous sculptor. And after much thought and discussion, the new statue was finally completed.

"Sister, is it all right?" asked the Superior anxiously. "Does it really look like the Blessed Virgin?"

Sister Catherine hesitated. The statue was beautiful—yes. Our Lady's dress was the soft, golden white of the sky just before dawn. Her eyes, raised to heaven as she offered the world to God, were alive with tenderness and love. But as for resembling Our Lady. . . .

"No, Mother. It doesn't look like her at all," she said quietly.

The Superior's face fell. "But Sister! The artist says it's the finest statue he's ever made! He's going to be so disappointed that you don't like it!"

Sister Catherine smiled, while a wave of compassion filled her heart. The poor artist! Certainly it wasn't his fault that the statue did not look like Our Lady. What human eye could ever capture her beauty, what hand describe it?

"Mother, please tell him everything's all right," she said hastily. "The statue is very beautiful."

"But you said. . . ."

"I know. But the poor man has done his best. I'm sure Our Lady is pleased. And I'm also sure she'll grant many graces to everyone who prays before the statue. After all, isn't that the real reason she wanted it made?"

The Mother Superior nodded slowly. "Yes, Sister. I suppose it is." But even as she spoke, her mind was busy with one thought. All who had seen the artist's work agreed that the new statue was most inspiring. It could move even the hardest heart to awe and reverence. Yet to Sister Catherine it fell so far short of Our Lady's beauty. . . .

"How lovely she must really be!" she reflected. "How incredibly beautiful! And easy to love!"

The many visitors who came to see the statue were of the same opinion. As for the Daughters of Charity, they naturally looked with new respect on the Sister who had made both statue and medal possible, and did all that they could to relieve the pains of her old age.

"To think she was the one who saw Our Lady!" they told one another in astonishment. "And we never even guessed it because she's always seemed so . . . well, ordinary!"

There was a good deal of discussion on this point. Yes, Sister Catherine *was* ordinary. In all the forty-six years of her religious life, she had never called attention to herself in the slightest way. She had done her work quietly and carefully, content to be just what God wanted her to be—an unknown soul obedient to His every wish.

Soon, even outside the convent, a number of people were trying to follow in Sister Catherine's footsteps. The truth which her humble life had so suddenly revealed to them—that holiness is not so much a matter of long prayers and great sacrifices as it is of giving oneself completely into God's hands for Him to do with as He wills—had touched their hearts. What did it matter that probably the only work He would ever ask of many of them would be to raise a family, suffer certain pains, perhaps just to earn a living for themselves? They all realized the same thing: that the secret of being a saint was first to give themselves to God *completely*, just as Sister Catherine had done, then wait in loving confidence for Him to make known His Will.

"If only everyone could understand this!" they told one another earnestly. "Even the children!"

"*Even the children?*" exclaimed Sister Catherine with a smile when she heard about the remark. "Why, it's really the children who can teach the rest of us how to give ourselves to God!"

Then, sick and feeble though she was, and confined to bed for most of the day, she began to explain to the Sisters who had come to see her just what she meant.

For instance, years ago Father Aladel had founded the Association of the Children of Mary. At first only girls had been members, but later boys had been admitted. Without exception, these young people had been taught to have a great devotion to Our Lady. They had been given the Miraculous Medal to wear about their necks, and encouraged to look upon the Blessed Virgin as their best friend. They had been urged to pray to her "for the graces for which people forget to ask,"—especially the grace to love God as she had loved Him when she was their age. But why? What was the real reason for devotion to Our Lady? For the Miraculous Medal itself?

"Isn't it so that we may learn to give ourselves to God completely, just as Our Lady did, and so start to become holy?" she demanded eagerly. "Oh, Sisters! I haven't lived for seventy years without discovering that usually it's the children who know how to do this best of all!"

Some of those present were quite puzzled by this statement. "Children?" they repeated curiously. "But Sister Catherine! Why should they find it . . . well, easier to be holy than anyone else?"

"Because most of them haven't yet learned to be really selfish," replied Sister Catherine calmly. "They're not like so many older people—afraid of God, or of what He may ask of them. They're only too glad to be tools in His service, if someone shows them how. The one trouble is. . . ."

"Yes, Sister?"

"Too few children are ever shown how. They grow up without ever knowing about giving themselves to God. Or the part Our Lady has to play in

"DISTRIBUTE THE MEDAL . . . IT WILL MEAN SO MUCH!"

helping them to be saints, especially when they wear her medal."

Then, worn though she was, and scarcely able to speak above a whisper, Sister Catherine made an earnest request of the Sisters gathered about her. When she was dead (and she would survive no longer than December 31 of that same year—1876), would they do all in their power to promote devotion to the Miraculous Medal among the boys and girls of their acquaintance? Would they tell them how Our Lady, the greatest of all the saints, had given herself to God when she was very young for Him to do with as He pleased, and that she was eager to help them to do the same so that they might be really happy when they grew up?

"Of course, Sister. What else?"

Sister Catherine smiled. "Have the children explain all this to their families," she whispered. "Have them distribute the medal to as many older people as they can. It ... it will mean so much!"

Tears in their eyes, the Sisters looked at one another in silence. What a touching message! Why, it had more power in it than many a sermon!

"We'll do everything possible to help the children promote the Miraculous Medal," they promised. "And if there's something else you would like. . . ."

With a little sigh Sister Catherine closed her eyes. "No," she murmured happily. "That's all."

St. Meinrad, Indiana
Feast of the Motherhood of the Blessed Virgin Mary
October 11, 1949

NOTE ON
THE CANONIZATION
OF ST. CATHERINE LABOURÉ

The Cause of Sister Catherine Labouré was introduced at Rome in 1907, and on December 12 of that same year she was declared Venerable. On May 28, 1933, she was solemnly beatified by Pope Pius the Eleventh, and on July 27, 1947, she was officially declared a Saint of the Church by Pope Pius the Twelfth.

By the same author . . .

6 GREAT CATHOLIC BOOKS FOR CHILDREN

. . . and for all young people ages 10 to 100!!

1137 THE CHILDREN OF FATIMA—And Our Lady's Message to the World. 162 pp. PB. 15 Illus. Impr. The wonderful story of Our Lady's appearances to little Jacinta, Francisco and Lucia at Fatima in 1917.   11.00

1138 THE CURÉ OF ARS—The Story of St. John Vianney, Patron Saint of Parish Priests. 211 pp. PB. 38 Illus. Impr. The many adventures that met young St. John Vianney when he set out to become a priest.   13.00

1139 THE LITTLE FLOWER—The Story of St. Therese of the Child Jesus. 167 pp. PB. 24 Illus. Impr. Tells what happened when little Therese decided to become a saint.   11.00

1140 PATRON SAINT OF FIRST COMMUNICANTS—The Story of Blessed Imelda Lambertini. 85 pp. PB. 14 Illus. Impr. Tells of the wonderful miracle God worked to answer little Imelda's prayer.   8.00

1141 THE MIRACULOUS MEDAL—The Story of Our Lady's Appearances to St. Catherine Labouré. 107 pp. PB. 21 Illus. Impr. The beautiful story of what happened when young Sister Catherine saw Our Lady.   9.00

1142 ST. LOUIS DE MONTFORT—The Story of Our Lady's Slave. 211 pp. PB. 20 Illus. Impr. The remarkable story of the priest who went around help-ing people become "slaves" of Jesus through Mary.   13.00

1136 ALL 6 BOOKS ABOVE (Reg. 65.00)   THE SET: 52.00

Prices subject to change.

U.S. & CAN. POST./HDLG.: $1-$10, add $3;
$10.01-$25, add $5; $25.01-$50, add $6; $50.01-$75, add $7;
$75.01-$150, add $8; $150.01 or more, add $10.

At your Bookdealer or direct from the Publisher.
Toll Free 1-800-437-5876   **Fax 815-226-7770**

6 <u>MORE</u> GREAT CATHOLIC BOOKS FOR CHILDREN

. . . and for all young people ages 10 to 100!!

1200 SAINT THOMAS AQUINAS—The Story of "The Dumb Ox." 81 pp. PB. 16 Illus. Impr. The remarkable story of how St. Thomas, called in school "The Dumb Ox," became the greatest Catholic teacher ever. 8.00

1201 SAINT CATHERINE OF SIENA—The Story of the Girl Who Saw Saints in the Sky. 65 pp. PB. 13 Illus. The amazing life of the most famous Catherine in the history of the Church. 7.00

1202 SAINT HYACINTH OF POLAND—The Story of The Apostle of the North. 189 pp. PB. 16 Illus. Impr. Shows how the holy Catholic Faith came to Poland, Lithuania, Prussia, Scandinavia and Russia. 13.00

1203 SAINT MARTIN DE PORRES—The Story of The Little Doctor of Lima, Peru. 122 pp. PB. 16 Illus. Impr. The incredible life and miracles of this black boy who became a great saint. 10.00

1204 SAINT ROSE OF LIMA—The Story of The First Canonized Saint of the Americas. 132 pp. PB. 13 Illus. Impr. The remarkable life of the little Rose of South America. 10.00

1205 PAULINE JARICOT—Foundress of the Living Rosary and The Society for the Propagation of the Faith. 244 pp. PB. 21 Illus. Impr. The story of a rich young girl and her many spiritual adventures. 15.00

1206 ALL 6 BOOKS ABOVE (Reg. 63.00)   THE SET: 50.00

Prices subject to change.

U.S. & CAN. POST./HDLG.: $1-$10, add $3;
$10.01-$25, add $5; $25.01-$50, add $6; $50.01-$75, add $7;
$75.01-$150, add $8; $150.01 or more, add $10.

At your Bookdealer or direct from the Publisher.
Toll Free 1-800-437-5876   **Fax 815-226-7770**

8 <u>MORE</u> GREAT CATHOLIC BOOKS FOR CHILDREN

. . . and for all young people ages 10 to 100!!

1230 SAINT PAUL THE APOSTLE—The Story of the Apostle to the Gentiles. 231 pp. PB. 23 Illus. Impr. The many adventures that met St. Paul in the early Catholic Church. 15.00

1231 SAINT BENEDICT—The Story of the Father of the Western Monks. 158 pp. PB. 19 Illus. Impr. The life and great miracles of the man who planted monastic life in Europe. 11.00

1232 SAINT MARGARET MARY—And the Promises of the Sacred Heart of Jesus. 224 pp. PB. 21 Illus. Impr. The wonderful story of remarkable gifts from Heaven. Includes St. Claude de la Colombière. 14.00

1233 SAINT DOMINIC—Preacher of the Rosary and Founder of the Dominican Order. 156 pp. PB. 19 Illus. Impr. The miracles, trials and travels of one of the Church's most famous saints. 11.00

Prices subject to change.

Continued on next page . . .

At your Bookdealer or direct from the Publisher.
Toll Free 1-800-437-5876   **Fax 815-226-7770**

1234 KING DAVID AND HIS SONGS—A Story of the Psalms. 138 pp. PB. 23 Illus. Impr. The story of the shepherd boy who became a warrior, a hero, a fugitive, a king, and more. 11.00

1235 SAINT FRANCIS SOLANO—Wonder-Worker of the New World and Apostle of Argentina and Peru. 205 pp. PB. 19 Illus. Impr. The story of St. Francis' remarkable deeds in Spain and South America. 14.00

1236 SAINT JOHN MASIAS—Marvelous Dominican Gatekeeper of Lima, Peru. 156 pp. PB. 14 Illus. Impr. The humble brother who fought the devil and freed a million souls from Purgatory. 11.00

1237 BLESSED MARIE OF NEW FRANCE—The Story of the First Missionary Sisters in Canada. 152 pp. PB. 18 Illus. Impr. The story of a wife, mother and nun—and her many adventures in pioneer Canada. 11.00

1238 ALL 8 BOOKS ABOVE (Reg. 98.00) THE SET: 78.00

Get the Complete Set!! . . .

SET OF ALL 20 TITLES

by Mary Fabyan Windeatt

(Individually priced—226.00 Reg. set prices—180.00)

1256 THE SET OF ALL 20 . . . . Only 160.00

Prices subject to change.

U.S. & CAN. POST./HDLG.: $1-$10, add $3;
$10.01-$25, add $5; $25.01-$50, add $6; $50.01-$75, add $7;
• $75.01-$150, add $8; $150.01 or more, add $10.

At your Bookdealer or direct from the Publisher.
Toll Free 1-800-437-5876 **Fax 815-226-7770**

TAN BOOKS AND PUBLISHERS, INC.
P.O. Box 424
Rockford, Illinois 61105

If you have enjoyed this book, consider making your next selection from among the following . . .

The 33 Doctors of the Church. *Fr. Christopher Rengers, O.F.M. Cap.* 33.00
Pope Pius VII. *Prof. Robin Anderson* 16.50
St. Pius V. *Prof. Robin Anderson* 7.00
Life Everlasting. *Garrigou-Lagrange, O.P.* 16.50
Mother of the Saviour/Our Int. Life. *Garrigou-Lagrange* 16.50
Three Ages/Int. Life. *Garrigou-Lagrange. 2 vol.* 48.00
Ven. Francisco Marto of Fatima. *Cirrincione,* comp. 2.50
Ven. Jacinta Marto of Fatima. *Cirrincione* 3.00
St. Philomena—The Wonder-Worker. *O'Sullivan* 9.00
The Facts About Luther. *Msgr. Patrick O'Hare* 18.50
Little Catechism of the Curé of Ars. *St. John Vianney.* 8.00
The Curé of Ars—Patron Saint of Parish Priests. *Fr. B. O'Brien.* 7.50
Saint Teresa of Avila. *William Thomas Walsh* 24.00
Isabella of Spain: The Last Crusader. *William Thomas Walsh* 24.00
Characters of the Inquisition. *William Thomas Walsh* 16.50
Blood-Drenched Altars—Cath. Comment. on Hist. Mexico. *Kelley* 21.50
The Four Last Things—Death, Judgment, Hell, Heaven. *Fr. von Cochem.* 9.00
Confession of a Roman Catholic. *Paul Whitcomb.* 2.50
The Catholic Church Has the Answer. *Paul Whitcomb* 2.50
The Sinner's Guide. *Ven. Louis of Granada* 15.00
True Devotion to Mary. *St. Louis De Montfort* 9.00
Life of St. Anthony Mary Claret. *Fanchón Royer* 16.50
Autobiography of St. Anthony Mary Claret. 13.00
I Wait for You. *Sr. Josefa Menendez* 1.50
Words of Love. *Menendez, Betrone, Mary of the Trinity.* 8.00
Little Lives of the Great Saints. *John O'Kane Murray* 20.00
Prayer—The Key to Salvation. *Fr. Michael Müller.* 9.00
Passion of Jesus and Its Hidden Meaning. *Fr. Groenings, S.J..* 15.00
The Victories of the Martyrs. *St. Alphonsus Liguori* 13.50
Canons and Decrees of the Council of Trent. *Transl. Schroeder* 16.50
Sermons of St. Alphonsus Liguori for Every Sunday. 18.50
A Catechism of Modernism. *Fr. J. B. Lemius* 7.50
Alexandrina—The Agony and the Glory. *Johnston.* 7.00
Life of Blessed Margaret of Castello. *Fr. William Bonniwell* 9.00
The Ways of Mental Prayer. *Dom Vitalis Lehodey* 16.50
Catechism of Mental Prayer. *Simler.* 3.00
St. Francis of Paola. *Simi and Segreti.* 9.00
St. Martin de Porres. *Giuliana Cavallini.* 15.00
The Story of the Church. *Johnson, Hannan, Dominica.* 22.50
Hell Quizzes. *Radio Replies Press* 2.50
Indulgence Quizzes. *Radio Replies Press.* 2.50
Purgatory Quizzes. *Radio Replies Press.* 2.50
Virgin and Statue Worship Quizzes. *Radio Replies Press* 2.50
Meditation Prayer on Mary Immaculate. *Padre Pio* 2.50
Little Book of the Work of Infinite Love. *de la Touche.* 3.50
Textual Concordance of The Holy Scriptures. *Williams.* pb. 35.00
Douay-Rheims Bible. *Paperbound.* 35.00
The Way of Divine Love. *Sister Josefa Menendez* 21.00
The Way of Divine Love. (pocket, unabr.). *Menendez.* 12.50
Mystical City of God—Abridged. *Ven. Mary of Agreda* 21.00

Prices subject to change.

Visits to the Blessed Sacrament. *St. Alphonsus* 5.00
Moments Divine—Before the Blessed Sacrament. *Reuter* 10.00
Miraculous Images of Our Lady. *Cruz* 21.50
Miraculous Images of Our Lord. *Cruz* 16.50
Raised from the Dead. *Fr. Hebert* 18.50
Love and Service of God, Infinite Love. *Mother Louise Margaret* 15.00
Life and Work of Mother Louise Margaret. *Fr. O'Connell* 15.00
Autobiography of St. Margaret Mary. 7.50
Thoughts and Sayings of St. Margaret Mary 6.00
The Voice of the Saints. *Comp. by Francis Johnston* 8.00
The 12 Steps to Holiness and Salvation. *St. Alphonsus* 9.00
The Rosary and the Crisis of Faith. *Cirrincione & Nelson* 2.00
Sin and Its Consequences. *Cardinal Manning* 9.00
St. Francis of Paola. *Simi & Segreti* 9.00
Dialogue of St. Catherine of Siena. *Transl. Algar Thorold* 12.50
Catholic Answer to Jehovah's Witnesses. *D'Angelo* 13.50
Twelve Promises of the Sacred Heart. (100 cards). 5.00
Life of St. Aloysius Gonzaga. *Fr. Meschler* 13.00
The Love of Mary. *D. Roberto* 9.00
Begone Satan. *Fr. Vogl* 4.00
The Prophets and Our Times. *Fr. R. G. Culleton* 15.00
St. Therese, The Little Flower. *John Beevers* 7.50
St. Joseph of Copertino. *Fr. Angelo Pastrovicchi.* 8.00
Mary, The Second Eve. *Cardinal Newman* 4.00
Devotion to Infant Jesus of Prague. *Booklet* 1.50
Reign of Christ the King in Public & Private Life. *Davies* 2.00
The Wonder of Guadalupe. *Francis Johnston* 9.00
Apologetics. *Msgr. Paul Glenn.* 12.50
Baltimore Catechism No. 1 . . . . 5.00
Baltimore Catechism No. 2 . . . . 7.00
Baltimore Catechism No. 3 . . . . 11.00
An Explanation of the Baltimore Catechism. *Fr. Kinkead.* 18.00
Bethlehem. *Fr. Faber* 20.00
Bible History. *Schuster.* 16.50
Blessed Eucharist. *Fr. Mueller* 10.00
Catholic Catechism. *Fr. Faerber.* 9.00
The Devil. *Fr. Delaporte* 8.50
Dogmatic Theology for the Laity. *Fr. Premm* 21.50
Evidence of Satan in the Modern World. *Cristiani* 14.00
Fifteen Promises of Mary. (100 cards). 5.00
Life of Anne Catherine Emmerich. 2 vols. *Schmoeger* 48.00
Life of the Blessed Virgin Mary. *Emmerich* 18.00
Manual of Practical Devotion to St. Joseph. *Patrignani* 17.50
Prayer to St. Michael. (100 leaflets) 5.00
Prayerbook of Favorite Litanies. *Fr. Hebert* 12.50
Preparation for Death. (Abridged). *St. Alphonsus* 12.00
Purgatory Explained. *Schouppe* 16.50
Purgatory Explained. (pocket, unabr.). *Schouppe* 12.00
Fundamentals of Catholic Dogma. *Ludwig Ott* 27.50
Spiritual Conferences. *Faber* 18.00
Trustful Surrender to Divine Providence. *Bl. Claude* 7.00
Wife, Mother and Mystic. *Bessieres* 10.00
The Agony of Jesus. *Padre Pio.* 3.00

Prices subject to change.

Seven Capital Sins. *Benedictine Sisters* 3.00
Confession—Its Fruitful Practice. *Ben. Srs.* 3.00
Sermons of the Curé of Ars. *Vianney* 15.00
St. Antony of the Desert. *St. Athanasius* 7.00
Is It a Saint's Name? *Fr. William Dunne* 3.00
St. Pius V—His Life, Times, Miracles. *Anderson* 7.00
Who Is Therese Neumann? *Fr. Charles Carty.* 3.50
Martyrs of the Coliseum. *Fr. O'Reilly.* 21.00
Way of the Cross. *St. Alphonsus Liguori* 1.50
Way of the Cross. *Franciscan version* 1.50
How Christ Said the First Mass. *Fr. Meagher.* 21.00
Too Busy for God? Think Again! *D'Angelo* 7.00
St. Bernadette Soubirous. *Trochu* 21.00
Pope Pius VII. *Anderson* 16.50
Treatise on the Love of God. 1 Vol. *de Sales. Mackey, Trans.* 27.50
Confession Quizzes. *Radio Replies Press* 2.50
St. Philip Neri. *Fr. V. J. Matthews.* 7.50
St. Louise de Marillac. *Sr. Vincent Regnault* 7.50
The Old World and America. *Rev. Philip Furlong* 21.00
Prophecy for Today. *Edward Connor* 7.50
The Book of Infinite Love. *Mother de la Touche* 7.50
Chats with Converts. *Fr. M. D. Forrest.* 13.50
The Church Teaches. *Church Documents* 18.00
Conversation with Christ. *Peter T. Rohrbach* 12.50
Purgatory and Heaven. *J. P. Arendzen.* 6.00
Liberalism Is a Sin. *Sarda y Salvany* 9.00
Spiritual Legacy of Sr. Mary of the Trinity. *van den Broek* 13.00
The Creator and the Creature. *Fr. Frederick Faber* 17.50
Radio Replies. 3 Vols. *Frs. Rumble and Carty* 48.00
Convert's Catechism of Catholic Doctrine. *Fr. Geiermann* 5.00
Incarnation, Birth, Infancy of Jesus Christ. *St. Alphonsus* 13.50
Light and Peace. *Fr. R. P. Quadrupani* 8.00
Dogmatic Canons & Decrees of Trent, Vat. I. *Documents* 11.00
The Evolution Hoax Exposed. *A. N. Field* 9.00
The Primitive Church. *Fr. D. I. Lanslots.* 12.50
The Priest, the Man of God. *St. Joseph Cafasso* 16.00
Blessed Sacrament. *Fr. Frederick Faber* 20.00
Christ Denied. *Fr. Paul Wickens* 3.50
New Regulations on Indulgences. *Fr. Winfrid Herbst* 3.00
A Tour of the Summa. *Msgr. Paul Glenn* 22.50
Latin Grammar. *Scanlon and Scanlon* 18.00
A Brief Life of Christ. *Fr. Rumble* 3.50
Marriage Quizzes. *Radio Replies Press* 2.50
True Church Quizzes. *Radio Replies Press.* 2.50
The Secret of the Rosary. *St. Louis De Montfort.* 5.00
Mary, Mother of the Church. *Church Documents* 5.00
The Sacred Heart and the Priesthood. *de la Touche* 10.00
Revelations of St. Bridget. *St. Bridget of Sweden* 4.50
Magnificent Prayers. *St. Bridget of Sweden* 2.00
The Happiness of Heaven. *Fr. J. Boudreau.* 10.00
St. Catherine Labouré of the Miraculous Medal. *Dirvin* 16.50
The Glories of Mary. *St. Alphonsus Liguori* 21.00
The Three Ways of the Spiritual Life. *Garrigou-Lagrange, O.P.* 7.00

Prices subject to change.

St. Vincent Ferrer. *Fr. Pradel, O.P.* 9.00
The Life of Father De Smet. *Fr. Laveille, S.J.* 18.00
Glories of Divine Grace. *Fr. Matthias Scheeben* 18.00
Holy Eucharist—Our All. *Fr. Lukas Etlin* 3.00
Hail Holy Queen (from *Glories of Mary*). *St. Alphonsus* 9.00
Novena of Holy Communions. *Lovasik* 2.50
Brief Catechism for Adults. *Cogan.* 12.50
The Cath. Religion—Illus./Expl. for Child, Adult, Convert. *Burbach* 12.50
Eucharistic Miracles. *Joan Carroll Cruz.* 16.50
The Incorruptibles. *Joan Carroll Cruz* 16.50
Secular Saints: 250 Lay Men, Women & Children. PB. *Cruz.* 35.00
Pope St. Pius X. *F. A. Forbes* 11.00
St. Alphonsus Liguori. *Frs. Miller and Aubin* 18.00
Self-Abandonment to Divine Providence. *Fr. de Caussade, S.J.* 22.50
The Song of Songs—A Mystical Exposition. *Fr. Arintero, O.P.* 21.50
Prophecy for Today. *Edward Connor* 7.50
Saint Michael and the Angels. *Approved Sources* 9.00
Dolorous Passion of Our Lord. *Anne C. Emmerich.* 18.00
Modern Saints—Their Lives & Faces, Book I. *Ann Ball.* 21.00
Modern Saints—Their Lives & Faces, Book II. *Ann Ball* 23.00
Our Lady of Fatima's Peace Plan from Heaven. *Booklet.* 1.00
Divine Favors Granted to St. Joseph. *Père Binet.* 7.50
St. Joseph Cafasso—Priest of the Gallows. *St. John Bosco.* 6.00
Catechism of the Council of Trent. *McHugh/Callan.* 27.50
The Foot of the Cross. *Fr. Faber.* 18.00
The Rosary in Action. *John Johnson* 12.00
Padre Pio—The Stigmatist. *Fr. Charles Carty* 16.50
Why Squander Illness? *Frs. Rumble & Carty* 4.00
The Sacred Heart and the Priesthood. *de la Touche* 10.00
Fatima—The Great Sign. *Francis Johnston* 12.00
Heliotropium—Conformity of Human Will to Divine. *Drexelius* 15.00
Charity for the Suffering Souls. *Fr. John Nageleisen* 18.00
Devotion to the Sacred Heart of Jesus. *Verheylezoon* 16.50
Who Is Padre Pio? *Radio Replies Press* 3.00
The Stigmata and Modern Science. *Fr. Charles Carty* 2.50
St. Anthony—The Wonder Worker of Padua. *Stoddard.* 7.00
The Precious Blood. *Fr. Faber* 16.50
The Holy Shroud & Four Visions. *Fr. O'Connell* 3.50
Clean Love in Courtship. *Fr. Lawrence Lovasik* 4.50
The Secret of the Rosary. *St. Louis De Montfort.* 5.00
The History of Antichrist. *Rev. P. Huchede.* 4.00
St. Catherine of Siena. *Alice Curtayne* 16.50
Where We Got the Bible. *Fr. Henry Graham* 8.00
Hidden Treasure—Holy Mass. *St. Leonard.* 7.50
Imitation of the Sacred Heart of Jesus. *Fr. Arnoudt* 18.50
The Life & Glories of St. Joseph. *Edward Thompson.* 16.50
Père Lamy. *Biver.* 15.00
Humility of Heart. *Fr. Cajetan da Bergamo* 9.00
The Curé D'Ars. *Abbé Francis Trochu* 24.00
Love, Peace and Joy. (St. Gertrude). *Prévot* 8.00

At your Bookdealer or direct from the Publisher.
Toll-Free 1-800-437-5876   **Fax 815-226-7770**

Prices subject to change.

MARY FABYAN WINDEATT

Mary Fabyan Windeatt could well be called the "storyteller of the saints," for such indeed she was. And she had a singular talent for bringing out doctrinal truths in her stories, so that without even realizing it, young readers would see the Catholic catechism come to life in the lives of the saints.

Mary Fabyan Windeatt wrote at least 21 books for children, plus the text of about 28 Catholic story coloring books. At one time there were over 175,000 copies of her books on the saints in circulation. She contributed a regular "Children's Page" to the monthly Dominican magazine, *The Torch*.

Miss Windeatt began her career of writing for the Catholic press around age 24. After graduating from San Diego State College in 1934, she had gone to New York looking for work in advertising. Not finding any, she sent a story to a Catholic magazine. It was accepted—and she continued to write. Eventually Miss Windeatt wrote for 33 magazines, contributing verse, articles, book reviews and short stories.

Having been born in 1910 in Regina, Saskatchewan, Canada, Mary Fabyan Windeatt received the Licentiate of Music degree from Mount Saint Vincent College in Halifax, Nova Scotia at age 17. With her family she moved to San Diego in that same year, 1927. In 1940 Miss Windeatt received an A.M. degree from Columbia University. Later, she lived with her mother near St. Meinrad's Abbey, St. Meinrad, Indiana. Mary Fabyan Windeatt died on November 20, 1979.

(Much of the above information is from Catholic Authors: Contemporary Biographical Sketches 1930-1947, ed. by Matthew Hoehn, O.S.B., B.L.S., St. Mary's Abbey, Newark, N.J., 1957.)